Jamestown REDISCOVERY V

William M. Kelso
Nicholas M. Luccketti
Beverly A. Straube

The Association for the Preservation
of Virginia Antiquities
1999

Dedication

William M. Kelso wishes to personally dedicate this booklet:
To Colonel Samuel Yonge, who was the first to follow documentary clues to sites on Jamestown Island, who was one of the few who thought some of James Fort's remains might have escaped river erosion, and who only missed predicting the exact position of James Fort by about a hundred feet.

To J. C. "Pinky" Harrington, 1901-1998, National Park Service retired, a man who will continue to inspire rigorous and insightful historical archaeology, a man who generously shared his enthusiasm for Jamestown, and a man who consistently and precisely recorded its archaeological record.

To Virginia Harrington, National Park Service retired, one of the few who really understands the role of "history" in historical archaeology and one of the few who believed James Fort remains might lie in the Jamestown churchyard.

Beverly A. Straube wishes to personally dedicate this booklet to her late father:
Edwyn (John) Warrell Mountain Hardy MBE, BEM, May 20, 1918-January 13, 1999, an English gentleman who, like many of the Jamestown colonists centuries before him, came to Virginia to find a better life.

Graphics by Jamie E. May
Design and production by Elliott Jordan

Printed in The United States of America

ISBN: 0-917565-07-X

Preface

Jamestown Rediscovery V is the fifth yearly booklet describing and interpreting the results of the James Fort excavations. As Virginia counts down to the year 2007 and the observance of the 400th anniversary of the founding of Jamestown, it is through these volumes and other media that the Association for the Preservation of Virginia Antiquities (APVA) continues its commitment to research *and* public education.

This work is generously funded by:

The Commonwealth of Virginia
The National Endowment for the Humanities
The National Geographic Society
Branches and members of the Association for the
Preservation of Virginia Antiquities

The success of *Jamestown Rediscovery* has come from the efforts of a great number of generous and talented people. Listing them all for the 1998 season alone is a monumental and worrisome task, monumental in the sense that several hundred individuals contributed to the field, lab, and interpretation of the project, and worrisome in the fact that someone will be mistakenly overlooked. When I do make that fatal and inevitable error of omission, I can only hope that those people, like me, really do not need thanks but rather get the most satisfaction from knowing that they were fortunate enough to have contributed something to the advancement of this unique and magical place called Jamestown.

I am extremely and continually grateful for the dedicated work of Beverly Straube, curator; Nicholas Luccketti, director of field projects; Elliott Jordan, information technologist and publisher; Jamie May, archaeologist/graphics designer; Eric Deetz, field supervisor; Seth Mallios, staff archaeologist; Michael Lavin, conservator and photographer; and Catherine Correll-Walls, office manager and research assistant. I am equally grateful to the Board and staff of the APVA, especially Martin Kirwan King, president; Peter Dun Grover, executive director; Elizabeth Kostelny, director of administration and finance; and the stalwart Jamestown volunteers. Special thanks to our Archaeological Advisory Board: Warren Billings, Dennis Blanton, Jeffrey P. Brain, Cary Carson, Kathleen Deagan, James Deetz, Rex Ellis, Alaric Faulkner, William Fitzhugh, Jon Kukla, David Orr, Oliver L. Perry, Sr., George Stuart, the late Wilcomb E. Washburn, Robert W. Wharton, Camille Hedrick, and Martha Williams; and for the cooperation of Alec Gould, Superintendent of Colonial National Historical Park, and his staff, particularly Diane

Stallings and Bill Warder. I am especially grateful for the expertise and generously donated time of Dr. Douglas Owsley of the National Museum of Natural History, Smithsonian Institution, and his staff who have instructed all of us in forensic anthropology. The skillful work of crew members Thad Pardue, Danny Schmidt, Camille Hedrick, Martha Gates, Heather Lapham and the APVA-University of Virginia Archaeological Field School directed by Garrett Fesler all made the 1998 summer field season outstanding. Charles Hodges is appreciated for sharing his fortification research. I am also especially grateful for the support and field labor of Governor James S. Gilmore and his family; first lady Roxane and their sons Jay and Ashton. Thanks also to Julie Grover, proofreader, and to Ellen, for her proofreading as well as her unwavering encouragement.

WMK 4/7/99

Before lending a hand to the excavation, Governor James S. Gilmore, first lady Roxane, and son, Jay, listen to Jamestown Rediscovery Director William Kelso explain the excavation of John White's warehouse at the James Fort site, July 1998.

Introduction

Jamestown Rediscovery

The Association for the Preservation of Virginia Antiquities' *Jamestown Rediscovery* Archaeological Project is primarily intended to be an ongoing series of discoveries of material and documentary survivals of early Jamestown life. The primary goal has been to uncover whatever survives of the James Fort/early James Town site before Virginia became a Royal Colony (1607-1624). That time period defines essentially a bicultural story of native Powhatan and immigrant Englishmen. Time did not, of course, stop in 1624. Therefore, the development of James Fort, the military settlement, into James Town, the commercial and political capital of a tobacco/slave-based agrarian colony, is another very significant focus of the *Jamestown Rediscovery* research.

Another APVA *Jamestown Rediscovery* goal, and perhaps equally as challenging as the primary research, is to involve the visiting public in the moment of discovering something new about the Jamestown past. But what does "discovery" really mean? First, it should be made clear the word "discovery" here is not used in the modern sense: someone finding something for the first time, as in "discovering" an unknown cave. The term is used as it was by navigators to the new world: to "investigate," "study," or "explore" some distant place heretofore unknown to the explorer. That is not to say that the distant place was unknown to everyone. In that sense, in 1607, Jamestown was "discovered" by Virginia Company men. Yet with the passing of almost four centuries, much about their "discovering," (what they experienced and the fabric of their material world) has become lost to modern memory and modern eyes. "Rediscovering" the material and documentary survivals of that early Jamestown then needs to be done. Moreover, the APVA believes that "rediscovery" of the nation's birthplace needs to be a shared experience, so much so that it becomes almost as much a current event for the visiting public at the Jamestown of the present as the Jamestown discovery process was for the original European settlers of the past. In that sense research archaeologists and the visiting public are the explorers (rediscoverers) of today.

Figure 1. Fragment of green-glazed English Border ware (1580-1610) found in the first Jamestown Rediscovery trench (April 1994) and intact drinking jug of the same ware type and date from the Fort dry moat.

Chapter 1

"…the saint-seeming worthies of Virginia"

It seemed to all work out so perfectly. The very first day of excavation produced a piece of "Tudor Green" pottery. I had just seen pots like that in the 16th- to early 17th-century galleries at the Museum of London. That quick return seemed like a good sign that 1607 James Fort had once stood somewhere near that first archaeological trench of the APVA's *Jamestown Rediscovery* project, begun on April 4, 1994, between the Jamestown church tower and the bank of the James River. But in all candor, I personally had tremendous misgivings as I, "staff" of one, started the digging. Conventional wisdom that the fort site, like Atlantis, had vanished long ago beneath the ravaging waves of the James was painfully convincing. Yet, a few skeptical scholars and I felt that someone had to find out what lay in the churchyard, whether it be nothing, the original English fort, or the remains of Jamestown from a later time. As I removed more and more dirt from that spot, it became clearer and clearer that someone from the James Fort era had once been there.

The spring of 1994 quickly turned to summer, and reinforcements, in the form of professional assistants and field school students, joined me at the site. As the blanket of plowed soil lifted, a dark streak in the subsoil proved to be a trench that once held upright side-by-side logs—a palisade wall! The next digging season revealed the telling signature of both a circular moat and palisade and another wall trench, striking an angle with the first that matched the best surviving eyewitness accounts of James Fort. The deposits associated with the palisades were just as important to this interpretation, containing over 150,000 artifacts, all old enough and military enough to be from the James Fort period. By the fall of 1996 we felt confident to announce to an enthusiastic and interested public that the lost James Fort was found!

It all seemed so easy. Of course nothing is. Sure enough, the 1998 season brought on puzzling twists. The digging uncovered a piece of the fort design far more intricate than a nice neat triangle. A backfilled pit containing military artifacts, trade goods, and domestic objects was found appended to the triangle by yet another palisade. Our first reaction was to hypothesize that the added palisade was part of the five-sided fortified town that Captain John Smith described as having been built soon after the devastating James Fort fire of 1608. But the palisade *appears* to only be about 50 feet long, ending a pedestrian gate's width from the "pit." Additional excavations revealed a set of circular steps into the pit, interior platforms at either end, evidence that a wooden wall once lined one side,

Figure 2. View of fort September 1998. Outwork palisade and cellar (foreground).

and a crude fireplace area on the earthen floor. This was obviously more than just a "pit;" it was a cellar. But the purpose of such a cellar and why it was filled in ca. 1610 with the same type of materials found in the other below-ground parts of James Fort was puzzling.

It is not uncommon for the archaeological process to turn up puzzles. Archaeologists can look to documents for possible answers to questions regarding Jamestown's inhabitants. The process often casts old records in

Figure 3. Overhead view of partially excavated outwork cellar showing stairs (left).

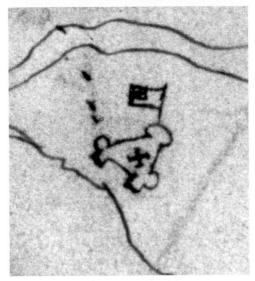

Figure 4. Section of 1608 Zuniga map with outworks on the southeast and southwest.

a new light. Historian Alexander Brown's 1890 two-volume *Genesis of the United States* contained an image of James Fort found in the archives of Spain.[1] It appeared to be a rough copy of a lost Captain John Smith map, depicting what is now northeastern North Carolina, extending north into present-day Virginia and Maryland to the head of the Chesapeake Bay. The map had been delivered to King Philip III by Pedro de Zuniga, Spanish ambassador to England, as part of a progress report to inform the King about the English encroachment into the *Spanish* New World. This map is significant to the history of Jamestown because it shows the only known plan of James Fort. The map depicts two complicated configurations of bastions on the southeastern and southwestern corners of the triangular fortification. It also shows what can be interpreted as an enclosed rectangular extension to the fort on the north, and a Maltese-like cross within the triangle oriented to the cardinal directions. The southeast corner of the fort plan shows a circular bastion to the east and a square bastion to the south. But the archaeological survival of the fort suggests an opposite plan, with a circular bastion to the south and a possible rectangular extension to the north.

What should we make of this apparent contradiction? Must we dismiss the archaeological evidence as incorrect? Not necessarily,—what is in the ground is in the ground. What is on paper can always be misread. It is possible that the map copier or even the original mapmaker, while accurately accounting for both a circular and square bulwark on the riverside corners of the fort, might for some reason have reversed them. However, before prematurely dismissing the map as flawed, it should be remembered that in other details the map and archaeological reality agree. In both cases the south wall of the triangle is oriented northwest to southeast of the compass-oriented cross. In fact, the cross almost certainly marks the location of the church, which by Christian tradition would be oriented east-west. If that is true, then future excavations in the area just east of the predicted center of the archaeological fort plan should uncover its remains.

Although the archaeology and the Zuniga map both verify the existence of rectangular-like palisaded projections, the purpose of these features is still unclear. The fact that a cellar was part of it provides little clarification. The fort, as it appeared to Colony Secretary William Strachey in July 1610, had gates at each angle of the triangle along with bulwarks and/or watchtowers.[2] If each angle had both a bulwark and a watchtower, then the rectangular projections of the Zuniga sketch seem to show us where they were located (albeit in reverse?). On the other hand, there is no indication that the cellar found archaeologically stood under any raised tower, though it is not yet fully excavated.

Smith might have left us a clue as to the cellar's function. In the winter of 1609, he reported:

"a pistol being stol'n and the thief fled, there was apprehended two proper young fellows that were brothers…now to regain this pistol the one was imprisoned, the other was sent to return the pistol again within twelve hours or his brother to be hanged. Yet the President [Smith] pitying the poor naked savage in the dungeon sent him victual and some charcoal for a fire. Ere midnight his brother returned with the pistol but the poor savage in the dungeon was so smothered with smoke he had made and so piteously burnt that we found him dead. The other most lamentable bewailed his death…that the president…told him that if hereafter they would not steal, he would make him alive again…with aqua vitae and vinegar, it pleased God to restore him again to life—but so drunk …he seemed lunatic…as much tormented the other as before to see him dead…laid by the fire to sleep which in the morning…had recovered…they went away… [and] spread among the savages that Captain Smith could make a man alive that was dead."[3]

Could the bulwark cellar be the Indian brother's dungeon? There was indeed evidence of a charcoal fire, the set of stairs appears to lead down from inside a palisade-protected space and there seems to be only one way in or out. Is this Jamestown's version of a solitary confinement cell relegated to the farthest reaches of the fort?

Figure 5. Engraving of "John Smith takes the King of the Pamaunke Prisoner, 1608."

Figure 6. Alternating fill probably from construction and "cleansing" of Jamestown in outwork cellar. Note steps in background left.

Dungeon or not, sometime in 1610 or shortly thereafter, the cellar and other below-ground *compartments* in or attached to the fort were filled. Initially a mixture of topsoil and subsoil clay wound up in each of the features, followed by solid layers of organic soil containing military and domestic garbage and trash. Because the first few layers were trash free, it appears that the dirt may have come from new construction. Conversely, the fact that the trash laden deposits were trash laden suggests they came from some major cleanup or nearby renovation campaign. It is also reasonably certain that the abandonment of the pits and the construction and/ or renovation took place at the same relative point in time. The nature and dates of the artifact collection recovered from the various pits were identical: arms, armor, and edged weapons; copper scrap and small objects made of copper, such as coins and tokens; small pots used in glass making (crucibles), drug jars, a variety of utilitarian camp kitchen and drinking related pottery; and the garbage bones of primarily wild animals and fish. Everything that could be dated with any precision either was made before 1610 or was known to have come to the colony during that year. Also, fragments from some of the same broken ceramic vessels turned up in all of the features. It is also important to point out that, based on the locations of the down-sloping layers in the pits, it is clear that the fill material primarily came from interior grounds of the fort. So the act of backfilling the pits was a result of related activity inside the palisade in or about 1610.

Why the relatively sudden construction/cleanup campaign? Again, perhaps the documentary eyewitness accounts offer explanation. First, con-

Figure 7. Excavation in the outwork cellar of an iron breastplate fashioned into a pail or cooking pot. This is one example of many where settlers converted "surplus" or otherwise ill-suited armor into other more useful objects (see figure 15).

sider the buildup of trash, and then its removal. John Smith tells us that whenever he was away from the fort, exploring or bartering for food, those left behind, because they were basically incompetent and/or lazy, allowed the place to degenerate. Of course, whether or not this was true each time Smith was gone is in some doubt. In his writings, he repeatedly portrays himself as the savior of the colony. Nevertheless, it is clear from multiple historical sources that soon after Smith left the colony permanently to seek medical help for a life-threatening wound, the fort turned into a ghetto. That was in the fall/winter of 1609-1610, "the starving time." By May 23, 1610, Strachey arrived to find this grim reality:

"our minister, Master Buck, made a zealous and sorrowful prayer finding all things...so full of misery and misgovernment...viewing the fort, we found the palisades torn down, the ports open, the gates from off the hinges, and empty houses (which owners death had taken from them) rent up and burnt,....And it is true, the Indian killed as fast without, if our men stirred but beyond the bounds of their blockhouse, as famine and pestilence did within...." [4]

Lord De La Warr, the new governor, found similar dreary conditions when he reached the Island and prevented the colony's desertion. Alexander Brown writes, "[De La Warre] landed at James' Town, being a very noisome and unwholesome place occasioned much by the mortality and idleness of our own people." But the new governor came with solutions for he quickly, "set the landsman…to cleanse the town."[5] This passage strongly suggests that De La Warr assigned a detail of the newly arrived and presumably energetic settler/soldiers to gather up the trash that had accumulated since May 13, 1607, and dispose of it. The organized and inspired new soldiers likely effected major repairs and redesigned the fort during this time, as well. This process would require digging new virgin soil and perhaps using it to fill in obsolete parts of the fort. By July 9-July 15, 1610, when Strachey wrote his most detailed description of the state of the fort, he could hint at these changes by prefacing his description, "…[James] fort, growing since [first construction] to more perfection, is now at present in this manner."[6] There is every reason to believe that future excavations will reveal what improvements replaced the below ground elements that brought the fort "to more perfection." For now, it seems archaeology in 1998 did indeed pose questions that gleaned more meaning from a Spanish spy map, a Captain Smith tale, and a new governor's revitalization program.

But could the nature of the rubbish gathered up by De La Warr's men tell us more about the planting of the colony? *Jamestown Rediscovery* is after all, more than an exercise in merely digging things up but rather an exercise in *historical* archaeology. This is a process that uncovers material Jamestown's past and endeavors to determine *why* those remains of the past wound up in the ground. The excavation part of the process is physical and clerical. The context and meaning part of the process is also physical and clerical but very historical. *Jamestown Rediscovery* is a constant interplay between the artifacts from the ground and the statements in period documents. A very significant part of the *Jamestown Rediscovery* historical archaeology process is its preoccupation with what appears to be minutiae. Much of its discoveries appear to be microscopic examination of trivia, over-focusing on the things of so little value that even the first settlers relegated them to the trash heap. If the process stopped at trash re-collection and then

Figure 8. Lord Governor De La Warr.

A Gentleman

Figure 9. An English Gentleman, 1610.

mere counting, the process would indeed be *just* an archaeological inventory and not particularly insightful. However the raw archaeological evidence is a direct link with an unfiltered material past, a past that just so happens to have a documentary account of it. Since historical documents detail many of these accounts, it is possible to transcend the trivial in insightful ways. Simply put, multiple lines of evidence—archaeological and historical—allow us to address *big* questions about the past.

For example, based on traditional historical interpretation, we might suppose that the beginnings of the United States, the world's sole remaining superpower, were in the hands of inept London businessmen. Out of touch with reality, they sent 104 of the most incompetent, lazy, and poorly equipped people in England to begin the British Colonial Empire on a mosquito-infested marshy peninsula that the local Algonquian Indians had abandoned as uninhabitable. It was only the importation of more people to replace the dead that enabled the hapless colony to take root. In other words, the Anglo-United States began as a greedy mistake and endured by coldly calculated human sacrifice. That may well be true. Since about half of the first settlers were listed as "gentlemen," it is logical to assume that they would be the least likely strata of English society to survive in a wilderness camp. It would have made far better sense, it would seem, to send hardy laborers and artisans skilled in the strenuous tasks that life in alien Virginia required. Smith continually complained about the poor suitability of his Virginia colleagues, writing "[they]…were poor gentleman, tradesmen, serving men, libertines…ten times more fit to spoil a commonwealth than either to begin one or but help to maintain one." About their ability to live with what nature provided, Smith offered, "Though there be fish in the sea, fouls in the air, and beasts in the woods their bounds are so large, they so wild and we so weak and ignorant we cannot much trouble them."[7] One could also conclude that Virginia Company officials knew little of the Virginia climate and, consequently, sent the wrong supplies. After all, wearing body armor in the blistering Virginia summer certainly could take a far greater toll on the population than the best Powhatan archer. And whatever food made it to the colonies would quickly spoil in the heat and humidity, as well. Overall, it is true that some of the Virginia colony officers and some of the adventurers made mistakes. But it does not necessarily follow that they all were undermining the success of the settlement. Recent archaeology suggests that there were more successes at Jamestown than Smith or assumptions regarding the predominance of gentlemen might lead one to believe.

The artifacts of early Jamestown are in many respects the "fallout" of the things people did there on a daily basis from May 13, 1607, to about 1611, that is, whenever they were periodically healthy or inspired enough to do anything at all. The archaeology reveals that they certainly did not do nothing. Specifically, the objects from the pit, moat, powder magazine, and dungeon clearly indicate that Jamestown was a very industrious place. Colonists, knowing the native desire for copper jewelry, fashioned trade goods into carefully designed forms. They were also experimenting with making glass, a commodity much needed in England. In addition, settlers were busy making "survival" products like shot, bullets, iron tools and implements from spare armor; repairing guns; and refining ore in search of precious metals. Of course, much time seems to have been required to hunt, fish, and repel frequent Indian guerrilla attacks. They were continually cutting down trees for palisades and to support houses. It is also clear that a number of people were doing a fair amount of digging: excavating clay pits, digging slot trenches for planting and/or repairing palisade timbers, digging postholes for the major timber supports for houses, excavating cellars for the powder magazine and a dungeon, and making coffins and digging graves. Many of the archaeological discoveries hint at images of an early Jamestown hard at work.

Figure 10. A collection of copper scrap, English-made Powhatan jewelry, coins, and jettons recovered from 1610 contexts at James Fort. According to John Smith, these objects were invaluable for the Powhatan trade until illegal barter by visiting sailors devalued them.

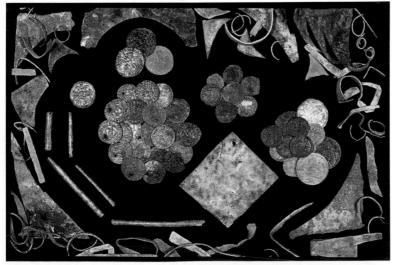

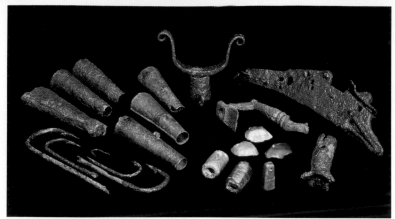

Figure 11. The settlers clearly had the equipment to hunt and fish for their own provisions, including various sizes of fishing hooks, lead net sinkers, firearms, and cylindrical powder containers.

Eyewitness descriptions of life at early Jamestown detail other activities that kept the colonists busy, as well. For instance, the men cut much timber for clapboarding and wainscoting, and dug and collected sassafras roots and "gilded" soil to relade the homeward bound ships in an effort to turn a profit for the sponsoring Virginia Company. Settlers also pitched tents and built houses and collected bark or reeds to cover them and built two blockhouses nearby the fort. The church and the store seemed to be continually under repair or in rebuilding. And on special days they would attend church or court or entertain a visiting emissary from the Powhatan chiefdom. Colonists bargained with seaman for food and whatever luxuries they could get their hands on when there was a supply ship in port. They also cleared fields and planted crops, with varying degrees of success, and attempted to raise horses, cows, hogs, goats, sheep, and chickens. The English drilled with their arms, took target practice, stood watch, and mounted ordinance. Thus, some were not idle. It is true that Captain John Smith lamented that certain gentlemen were not only not aiding the

Figure 12. The men at James Fort spent much time making their own bullets and shot as the bullet molds, various sizes of balls, and drip shot suggest.

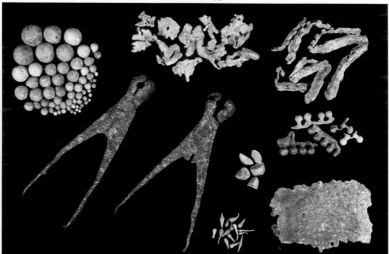

Figure 13. Some of the men at James Fort were clearly conducting experiments in making small trials of glass leaving behind stoneware crucibles still containing sand and melted glass and broken window glass cullet.

Figure 14. Finding precious metals in Virginia was a major goal of the Jamestown adventure. Artifacts from the Fort show evidence of assaying ores: crucible containing copper (above center), antimony (left), and zinc sulphide (right) fluxes used in separating precious metals. Earthenware distillation flask (below).

se of settlement, but in fact spending all their time black keteering and living high on the hog. These were the men he astically called "…the saint-seeming worthies of Virginia."[8] ers, say artifacts and documents, were hard at meaningful work. ese were the *saintly worthies* of Virginia. As a result of their ef- s, Jamestown would live on to become the first permanent En- settlement in the New World.

Figure 15. Fashioning armor into more useful things, like jack plates for the lighter iron-reinforced jacket and breastplates into containers, was another pastime of the James Fort men.

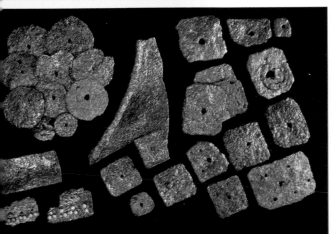

Figure 16. Overview of the James Fort/John White's site, September 1998.

Figure 17. Site map as of Fall 1998.

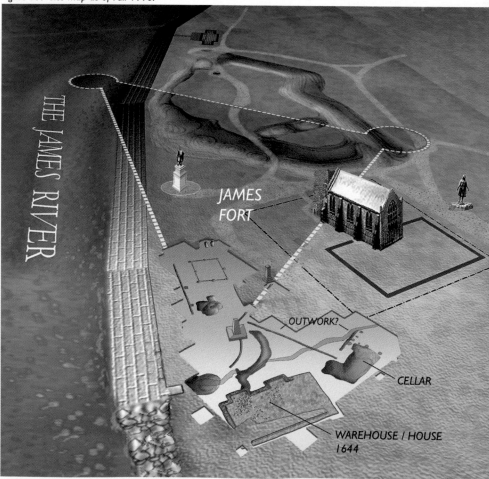

THE JAMES RIVER

JAMES FORT

OUTWORK?

CELLAR

WAREHOUSE / HOUSE 1644

Chapter 2
John White's Site

The 1998 excavation season focused on two major features: the back-filled cellar located at the end of the extended palisade trench (see Chapter 1) and the site of a masonry building foundation built adjacent to and directly on the site of the abandoned fort bulwark. Both of these features are major discoveries. Again, the palisade and cellar are contemporary with all of the parts of James Fort uncovered during past seasons, and therefore show that James Fort was not as neatly triangular as eyewitness descriptions have lead people to believe. The building foundation, while built after the Fort ceased to exist, is equally significant. It symbolizes Jamestown's evolution from military camp of the first years of settlement to commercial river port/Virginia capital in the second quarter of the 17th century. The building was almost certainly built and used by merchant, politician, planter and land speculator, John White.

As excavation in 1996 uncovered more of the backfilled fort moat toward the east, it soon became apparent that construction of a later masonry building cut into the moat. Excavation during the 1998 season exposed more of the building remains. Judged by Jamestown standards, the foundation is massive. It measures 30' wide and 50' long overall with two

Figure 18. View of the John White's site ruin. This is an undistorted mosaic of the remains produced by combining a number of overhead views taken at the same measured distance. View facing west.

exterior chimney foundations asymmetrically spaced along the west wall. The main wall remains indicate that the building stood on a sizable cobblestone footing; however, very little of the stones remain in place. Removal of the plowed overburden and some clay backfill inside the wall line revealed two concentrations of brick rubble: mortared sections of fallen chimney stacks and leftover bricks probably thrown there by building material salvors. Most of the bricks are normal-sized red to orange building bricks, but there are a considerable number of pale yellow undersized "Dutch" bricks and orange undersized English paving bricks, as well. The smaller bricks were concentrated at each hearth and in the southwestern corner of the building. Except for a line of the English pavers along the hearth line of the south chimney, these undersized bricks seem to have been piled and abandoned by the brick salvors where they were found. A number of curved (pan tile) roofing tiles were also identified in the interior rubble. The use of Dutch bricks and a tile roof suggest that this was a building of some quality.

There are areas of the building interior free of brick rubble, one on the south is of particular significance. There, removal of the overburden exposed a section of charred wooden flooring. The elevation of the floor indicates that at least the south side of the building had only a partially below-grade English basement. The charcoal also seems to establish that the entire building was destroyed by fire. A burned timber threshold was also found laying in what appears to be an oversize door at the center of the south wall. This marks what was almost certainly a cargo door facing the river landing.

Figure 19. John White's north chimney foundation showing partially salvaged "Dutch" bricks, the smaller English paving bricks, and some unsalvaged cobblestone foundation (foreground).

When the building stood and when it burned is still unknown. One early exploratory excavation in the interior of the south fireplace recovered no artifacts to date the deposit. No other prefire levels and no more of the fire and occupation levels have yet been excavated. However, discovery of a ditch "zigzagging" across the James Fort bastion site indirectly gives some clues to the life span of the building and probably identifies the builder. The location of the ditch leaves little doubt that it marked a property line separating the churchyard from private land. That private land must have once belonged to a John White who patented land at James City described as follows:

> "one Acre of Land lyeing in James Citty bounded west upon the Church Yard East upon the Land apprtaining to the State house North towards the Land of mr Thomas Hampton, and south upon James river the Length being Twenty three poles and the breadth seven poles almost." [9]

Beyond establishing the owner, the patent also may answer the question about the extent of Jamestown shoreline erosion, at least in the area south of the church since 1644. Based on terms used in other Jamestown patents, "breadth" meant the width of the property at the river shore. So the north and south boundaries were the shortest, 115.5', or 7 poles (16.5' each). Conversely the east and west boundaries of the property were the "length" measurements, and they were therefore 379.5' from river shore to the north property line. In that case, and if no erosion occurred over the past 355 years (1644-1999), then the zigzag trench should still measure 379.5' long from river bank to lot corner. Anything short of that distance would establish how much shoreline is gone. While the 1998 excavations did not trace the entire line, two spot trench tests suggest that it is at least 200' long and still going. The current testing also determined that the trench would have to be traced continuously to be sure that the terminus point is the true northern extent of the property. That excavation is planned for the future.

Figure 20. Burned floorboards and in situ nails near south chimney, John White's.

Figure 21. Posthole and aligned brick step(?)—possibly remains of a pier or loading platform associated with John's White's building.

Two large and deep postholes and associated aligned brick were found extending from the southwest corner of the foundation. Each posthole once held a sizable timber. They may have supported the north wall of an addition to the building, the full plan of which may still be found by excavation between the postholes and the seawall. It is also possible that the posts supported some type of loading dock extending toward the water or anchored a pier that extended offshore. It is possible that the post construction predates the building in that it extends over the boundary line to the west. Further interpretation depends on future excavation.

It is too soon to try to imagine what the building may have looked like in elevation. There is a possible lead, however. A building this large and the fact that White was a merchant suggest that it was a warehouse and a house combined. Good examples still stand in Ipswich, Suffolk, owned and operated by merchants for centuries, and at King's Lynn, Norfolk, where Captain John Smith held a brief apprenticeship. Both of these buildings doubled as the merchant's house and, as they extended to the water's edge, provided warehouse space, as well. The plan of the foundation also suggests that it had more than a single gable roof. Perhaps the 16th-century custom's house in the West Country river port town of Topsham, Devon, is an English precedent. A Dutch chart of the "Powhatan River" recently discovered at the Hague shows Jamestown and a symbol of a long building with a roof of three gables.[10] The building is located on Jamestown Island in about the same place as White's property. There is reason to believe that the map information was gathered in 1617 and drawn in the 1630s, while White's patent requires him to build on his new property within six

Figure 22. Wool merchant's house (background) now known as the Isaac Lord house/warehouse, Ipswich, England, first built 1530-1550, remolded in 1636, stands north of an attached early 17th-century salesroom/warehouse, possibly the same type of structure as John White's.

Figure 23. Triple-gabled 16th-century customs house, Topsham, England (above), and detail of Jamestown Island from a Dutch Chart drawn after 1617.

months after the patent date of August 28, 1644. It is impossible that the building foundation of the 1630s shown on the chart could be White's building built a decade later. However, the chart depiction house does suggest that this type of structure may have been a Jamestown house/warehouse prototype.

Even though the name is almost as common as John Smith, there are enough documentary references to apparently the same John White from the 1640s and 1650s to give him a biography. If these are references to the same man, his resume suggests what might have been a typical multifaceted Jamestown entrepreneur. In 1642 John White served in the House of Burgesses.[11] He was a merchant of London *and* Virginia and in 1649 sold the land that ultimately became the site of modern downtown Richmond.[12] He also grew and shipped tobacco.[13] If White's commingled enterprises were as typical as they appear, then apparently "the business of America is business" has always been so.[14]

Jamestown Rediscovery's dual goals, unearthing the Jamestown story and sharing those discoveries in "real time" with the public, requires innovative techniques. To those ends, the John White building foundation has become an exhibition excavation, protected by an aluminum-framed fabric dome. Fully protected from the elements, the building remains will be slowly exposed as a demonstration of discovery, connecting the viewing public directly with the remnants of the Jamestown past, a layer at a time. The first goal is to exhibit the ruins as they appeared at the moment in time when brick salvors scavenged the burned ruin, probably ca. 1650. In future seasons, fire, occupation, and construction levels will go on view. At the same time, this site will be an experiment in archaeological site excavation, recording, preservation, and education.

Figure 24. Archaeological pavilion protecting John White's building foundation excavation east of James Fort site.

Chapter 3

by Nicholas Luccketti

The Road to James Fort

"...in the hope that part of James Fort still stood on the dry land..."

Joel Shiner, 1955 [15]

On Monday, February 14, 1955, Jamestown National Park Service (NPS) archaeologist Joel Shiner and two workers peeled off the sod from an exploratory trench between the James River and the Confederate Fort. This marked the beginning of Project 100, the NPS's three-month search on the APVA's Jamestown Island property for physical remains of the first permanent English settlement in the New World. In the 1950s, the study of 17th-century Virginia fortifications was in its infancy. Jamestown archaeologists at that time, J.C. "Pinky" Harrington, John Cotter, and Joel Shiner all were true pioneers who plunged into the wilderness of early colonial fortifications when the only American forts of that period known archaeologically were both earthworks. In retrospect, the earthen walls of the 1580s Fort Raleigh on Roanoke Island, North Carolina, [16] and John Smith's 1609 "new Forte" in Surry County, Virginia, [17] blinded rather than enlightened these archaeologists. For example, when Pinky Harrington supervised the excavation of a proposed sewer line on APVA property in 1949, he found postholes and a sec-

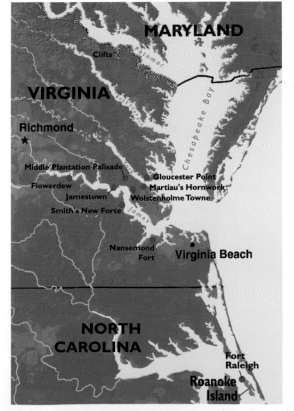

Figure 25. Location of 17th-century fortified sites.

tion of a 1' wide ditch not far from the seawall south of the Jamestown Church. He thought these features represented nothing more than ordinary 17th-century fencelines like those that had been excavated at Jamestown in the 1930s.[18] In 1949, Harrington had no reason to think otherwise. Nevertheless, the consummate professional archaeologist, Harrington noted and precisely recorded these unimpressive features anyway. Years later, excavations by *Jamestown Rediscovery* revealed that this 1' wide trench actually was part of the riverside wall of James Fort.

Project 100's last exploratory trench was backfilled on June 7, 1955. Nearly four decades would pass before an APVA archaeological team returned to the Jamestown Church area to shovel, trowel, and screen soil

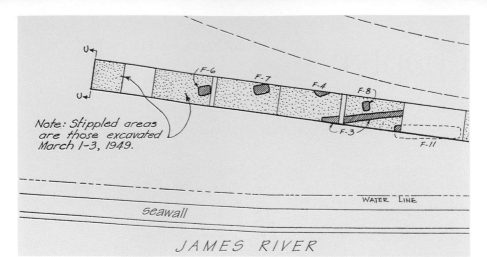

Note: Stippled areas are those excavated March 1-3, 1949.

seawall

WATER LINE

JAMES RIVER

Figure 26. Detail of Harrington's 1949 map of archaeological survey showing a section of the James Fort palisade trench.

in a renewed search for evidence of James Fort. During the interlude, Virginia archaeologists unearthed a host of fortified 17th-century sites throughout eastern Virginia, mainly in the lower Tidewater region. They learned that the majority of fortifications of that period were not thick walls of large tree-like posts with wide deep trenches, nor were they earthworks, but rather they were predominately palisades of light timbers set into shallow narrow trenches. These discoveries paved the way for archaeologists to reconsider the true nature of fort construction in early 17th-century Virginia. Ultimately, the knowledge gained from sites like the Clifts on the Potomac near Stratford Hall, the Nansemond Fort site on the south side of the James River in what is today the City of Suffolk, and Martiau's Hornwork at Yorktown enabled *Jamestown Rediscovery* archaeologists in the mid-1990s to recognize the often subtle but unmistakable traces of the slot trench palisades for the walls and southeast bulwark of the recently uncovered James Fort.

Figure 27. APVA President Ellen Bagby with J.C. Harrington and NPS staff during 1955 visit to Project 100.

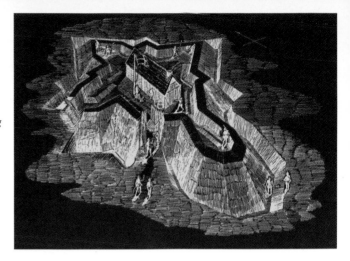

Figure 28. Conjectural drawing of Fort Raleigh earthwork.

Punches and Planks

The more than half dozen forts or sites with fortifications excavated since 1976 have taught archaeologists that two different methods of construction were used to build timber forts in 17th-century Virginia, punches and planks.[19] The most prevalent method of building wooden fortification walls was to place small timbers side by side into a narrow trench, generally about 1' wide, sometimes called a slot trench. This building technique was known as puncheon construction in the 17th century. "Punches" referred to slight and narrow timbers, as opposed to stout logs, that were either driven into the ground to make crude cabin-like buildings or set close together in a trench to create a palisade.[20] Slot trench palisade construction was used in all manner of fortifications from large forts, like Nansemond Fort and James Fort, to small forts protecting a single house as seen at the Clifts, and to barriers such as the 1630s Middle Plantation palisade that once linked College Creek on the James River to Queen's Creek Creek on the York River.

The ca. 1619 fort at Wolstenholme Towne, the core site of Martin's Hundred plantation in James City County, was the first and one of the earliest 17th-century timber forts discovered in Virginia, yet its post-rail-and-plank construction apparently was not widely employed in other

Figure 29. Conjectural painting of Wolstenholme Towne fort.

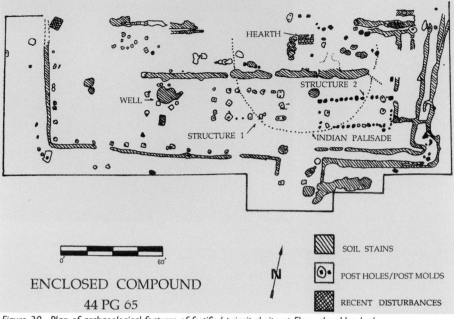

Figure 30. Plan of archaeological features of fortified principal site at Flowerdew Hundred.

fortifications.[21] The Wolstenholme Towne fort was a 130' long and 93' wide trapezoid with rectangular bastions projecting off at least two corners. The fort walls were built around posts spaced at 9' intervals with connecting horizontal rails which in turn were sheathed with vertical pales or planks. A shallow trench along the inside of the fort walls indicated the location of a firing platform which, in turn, suggested that the fort walls were at least 7'6" tall.

There are other 17th-century Virginia sites where timber defensive works may have been used, however, the archaeological footprint of the fortifications is too ambiguous to understand with certainty. Flowerdew Hundred plantation, established in 1619 by Sir George Yeardley along the south bank of the James River in Prince George County, is a good example.[22] Extensive archaeology around the ca. 1619-1630 central site has exposed clear evidence of some type of protective enclosure, but the jumble of ill-defined features is extremely difficult to puzzle out. Interpretations range from elaborate derivations of sophisticated European Renaissance fortifications[23] to a simple post-rail-and plank palisade.[24]

Nicolas Martiau's Hornwork

Prior to the onset of residential construction in the colonial village of Yorktown, an archaeological study of the construction area was commissioned by the developers in the spring of 1989.[25] The survey quickly showed that the area was extraordinarily rich with well-preserved archaeological remains mostly associated with Yorktown's well known 18th-century and Civil War history. Documentary research also revealed that the block was within the bounds of the first European landholder, Nicolas

Figure 31. Overhead view of excavation in Yorktown showing east half of hornwork.

Martiau. Martiau, a Huguenot born in 1591, was a trained military engineer in the service of the Earl of Huntington, who sent Martiau to Jamestown in 1620.[26] A Virginia Company of London meeting held on March 2 of that year reported the following:

> *"...touchinge the desyre of the Plantacon to be accomodated wth some Enginers att their owne charges for Raysing a fforteficacon, ...butt acquainted them of a ffrenchman who hath been longe in England very skillfull therin who pmised to agree wth him for a certaine some of monny to goe over and live there signefyinge of two sortes of ffortefycacons, one for the induringe of assaults and Battery, which is not as hee Accompts there very needful butt rather the other of chusinge and takinge some place of Advantage, and there to make some Pallysadoes wch hee conceiveth the fittest, and for wch this ffrenchman is singuler good."[27]*

The "singuler good" Frenchman was surely Nicolas Martiau.

Martiau received a grant in 1630 for 1300 acres along the south bank of the York River and settled in the immediate vicinity of present day Yorktown. He died in 1652, and 50 acres of the original landholding was sold by his descendants in 1691 for the construction of the new town of Yorke.

Figure 32. Detail of north end of Martiau's Hornwork showing palisade trench with gaps between posts.

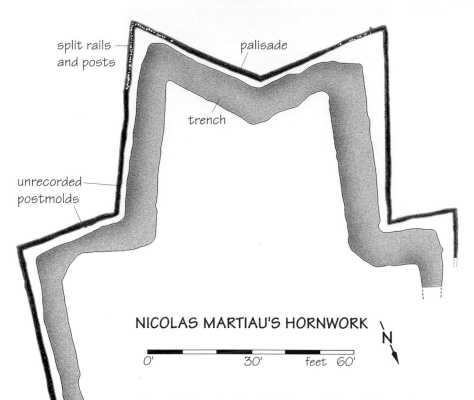

split rails
and posts

palisade

trench

unrecorded
postmolds

NICOLAS MARTIAU'S HORNWORK

N

0'   30'   feet 60'

Figure 33. Plan of archaeological features of Martiau's Hornwork.

Based on the extensive findings of the archaeological survey, the developers funded a major salvage excavation which unearthed a plethora of features, including Union and Confederate soldiers' huts, Revolutionary War soldiers' huts, an 18th-century kitchen/well/yard complex, and an 18th-century store. Beneath all these remains, each known to some degree through historical documents, was an anonymous, narrow clay-filled trench about 1½' wide that cut through the undisturbed old topsoil layer. The trench contained the dark loam stains of decomposed wooden posts. The narrow trench was sealed by all the 18th-century deposits and therefore preceded the establishment of the town of Yorke at the end of the 17th century. Fully uncovered, the trench outlined an irregular "star"-shaped pattern, recognizable as a type of fortification known as a hornwork. A hornwork was a formally designed strong point or outwork that was connected to the outer walls of a fort and a common feature of 17th-century European forts. Without doubt, the Yorktown hornwork must have been the creation of Nicolas Martiau and apparently was attached to the south end of a fort that was graded away decades ago.

The hornwork consisted of an exterior barrier constructed of small posts set, not driven, into a 1' wide slot trench. Significantly, the posts were separated by roughly 6" gaps and not set side-by-side, as in other palisades. Thus, this palisade cannot have been a tight wall and must have served as an obstacle. Two and a half feet inside the palisade was a parallel 8'-wide

Figure 34. Drafting compass extension found during hornwork excavation.

ditch that was 2' deep below subsoil. The bottom of the ditch was filled with a layer of sandy clay that sloped in from the inside of the hornwork; it clearly was the result of rain washing the soil off of an adjacent earthwork. Therefore, the hornwork consisted of a rampart fronted by an 8'-wide ditch which, in turn, was surrounded by a palisaded barrier. Standard military architecture of the period called for the construction of palisades on top of ramparts, as well. However, it is extremely unlikely that a rampart capping palisade would have been sufficiently deep to penetrate completely through the rampart into the subsoil to leave telltale soil stains.

The 45-degree angle of the points of the "M"-shaped part of the hornwork was formed by 56'-long outside legs and 40'-long inside legs. A 20' long wing or flank extended off the west side, while the east side had a 30'-long flank which turned north for 56' before it disappeared. One of the most intriguing artifacts recovered during the excavation was a 6"-long brass piece that proved to be an extension arm for a large compass. A compass was an essential instrument that enabled a military engineer to draft the required angles and proportions of a proper, European state-of-the-art fortification.

Nansemond Fort

The Nansemond Fort site was first discovered by contract archaeologists surveying farmland scheduled for development on the east side of the Nansemond River. A concentration of artifacts and oyster shells on the surface of a freshly plowed and rainwashed field betrayed the presence of an archaeological site. The artifacts told the archaeologists that the site dated to the second quarter of the 17th century, which coincided nicely with the time of the first English patents on the east side of the Nansemond River in ca. 1636. But, of course, the pottery sherds and fragments of tobacco pipes had nothing to say about the presence of a fort. It was no great surprise that the written record was equally silent on the Nansemond Fort; indeed, there was precious little information in the surviving documents about the fundamental history of the site, such as who lived there and when.[28] The first landowner most likely was John Wilkins, who, in 1636, patented 1,300 acres on the east side of the Nansemond River abutting Knott's Creek. Wilkins was living in Accomac County on Virginia's Eastern Shore in 1623 and likely never occupied his Nansemond

Figure 35. Overhead view of Nansemond Fort site.

River tract. Wilkins may have placed indentured servants or tenants on the property, but only for a short time, since the land was sold to Michael Wilcox by 1638. Wilcox, an "Ancient Planter" who came to Virginia in 1610 in De La Warr's fleet, apparently lived on his new holdings. Sometime before 1645, Wilcox died and his widow Elinor married Samuel Stoughton, a burgess, who repatented the land that formerly belonged to Michael Wilcox.

The excavation of the site by the Virginia Company Foundation (VCF) began in the summer of 1990.[29] Mechanical removal of the plowzone exposed a complex of typical 17th-century post-in-the-ground structures and refuse pits; all surrounded a 1' wide and 1' deep palisade trench creating the largest wooden fort ever found in Virginia. Nansemond Fort had a

Figure 36. Simplified archaeological plan of Nansemond Fort site.

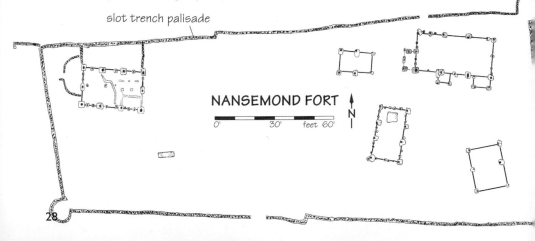

slot trench palisade

NANSEMOND FORT

0'   30'   feet 60'

N

trapezoidal plan just like the Wolstenholme Towne fort. Both were approximately the same width, 98' and 93', respectively. However, the south wall or curtain of Nansemond Fort was 222' long as compared to the 130' length of the Wolstenholme Towne fort.

Figure 37. Unexcavated northeast bastion of Nansemond Fort.

The Nansemond Fort walls were safeguarded by two rounded bastions at opposite ends of the fort. The larger northeast bastion was roughly 14' in diameter with a 5'6"-wide entrance or gorge, while the smaller southwest bastion, with a similar sized gorge, was 9½'-10' in diameter. The fort had two gates appearing as gaps in the palisade trench: a 4'-wide main gate in the south curtain and a 2½'-wide postern gate in the north curtain near the main dwelling of the settlement. The north wall of Nansemond Fort had a curious but deliberate 2'9" right-angle turn about 140' from the northeast bastion, and this jog may have been an additional protected position for musket fire along the north wall. The south wall also contained a similar jog 25' east of the main gate. There was no evidence that the fort had a firing step behind the walls nor that the bastions had elevated platforms for cannon. Thus it seems that Nansemond Fort was a breastwork whose walls were just tall enough for the defenders to shoot over.

Figure 38. Conjectural drawing of Nansemond Fort site.

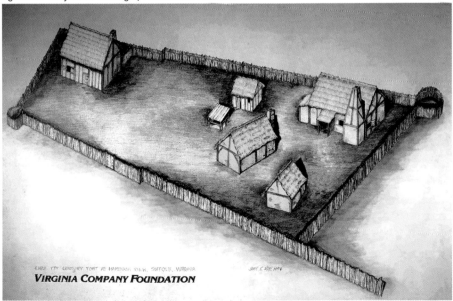

EARLY 17TH CENTURY FORT AT HAMPTON VIEW, SUFFOLK, VIRGINIA

VIRGINIA COMPANY FOUNDATION

Figure 39. Rectangular bastion under VIMS building at Gloucester Point.

Gloucester Point

In 1983, archaeologists with the Virginia Research Center for Archaeology (VRCA), were given a Herculean task. The Virginia Institute of Marine Science (VIMS), located at Gloucester Point directly across the river from Yorktown, intended to build a 90,000-square-foot academic building right in the heart of colonial Gloucester Town.[30] Given the well-documented presence of Gloucester Town and the near 200-year succession of fortifications built at the strategic narrows between Yorktown and Gloucester Point, it was little wonder that a VRCA survey of the planned construction area turned up a staggering number of archaeological remains. Consequently, a massive salvage excavation was launched. Working with a mostly volunteer field crew, the state archaeologists uncovered a bastion for a large Civil War fort, a Revolutionary War gun battery, a Revolutionary War cemetery, six Gloucester Town buildings, one pre-Gloucester Town basement, and mountains of colonial refuse. Within the maze of pits, postholes, ditches, and under a Civil War rampart, there were the telltale soil marks of three palisade trenches. The narrow trenches contained the soil stains of long decayed posts called postmolds. The 6"-diameter postmolds were set side by side and formed a 15' by 10' rectangle. The base of the rectangle was obliterated by a large Civil War fort trench, but enough of the southwest corner was sufficiently intact to show a palisade trench turning away from the open end of the rectangle. This almost certainly represents a bastion to a fort or fortified house dating to the 1640s or 1650s during the first years of settlement at Gloucester Point.[31]

The Clifts

Overlooking the south shore of the Potomac River, the Clifts was established around 1670 in Westmoreland County by Thomas Pope.[32] Pope's descendants later sold their land in 1718 to Thomas Lee who built Stratford Hall. Since Thomas Pope is known to have lived elsewhere on his 2400-acre tract, it seems that the Clifts site was a tenant farm. However, architectural and artifactual evidence suggest that the anonymous tenants were remarkably prosperous for their station. In 1675, tensions between English settlers in the Northern Neck and the neighboring Susquehannock Indians erupted into hostilities. Tangible evidence of this conflict was discovered in 1976 at the Clifts site when archaeologists found a slot trench palisade with bastions surrounding the manor house.

Figure 40. Plan of archaeological features for Clifts manor house and palisade.

The Clifts palisade was slightly trapezoidal and measured 55' by 60'. The 1'-wide palisade construction trench was dug 12"-18" deep into the subsoil which, added to the 13"-thick layer of plowzone that covered the subsoil, resulted in a palisade trench that was 2' to 2½' deep originally. The palisade walls were protected by two crudely circular bastions, each about 8' in diameter, and the fort had two gates marked by 3' and 4' gaps in wall lines. Meticulous excavation of the palisade revealed that the wooden uprights, which appeared as postmolds at the bottom of the trench, were not driven but set flat on the trench bottom. The postmolds were mostly triangular shaped, leading the archaeologists to conclude that the "punches" of the palisade were likely split rails from worm fences, a ready source of timbers recycled by the Clifts tenants during a time of crisis.[33]

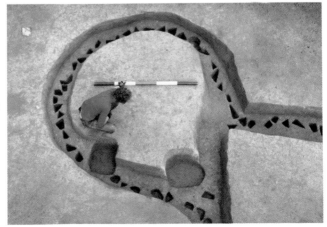

Figure 41. Northwest bastion at the Clifts showing triangular postmolds in palisade trench.

"Two Sortes of Ffortefycacons"

At first glance, the absence of experienced fort builders in Virginia seems odd given the inherent dangers of settling in the New World, but it is understandable in light of two things. First, professional military engineers were in great demand in 17ᵗʰ-century Europe and their services were at a premium, even in England. Virginia Company officials and General Sir Edward Cecil, the company's military consultant and one of the most famous generals of his day, faced this predicament in 1620. Even a man of Cecil's stature encountered severe difficulties in securing the services of a military engineer for Virginia because "…they beinge so exceedinge deare and hard to be gotten that they will not worke under five or six shillings a day." [34]

The second reason why the bulk of the early Virginia fortifications were not constructed by military engineers is that most of the 17ᵗʰ-century Virginia fortifications were directed at deterring Native American threats. It was not necessary for English colonists to build sophisticated geometri-cally-crafted timber forts or earthworks in order to defend themselves from the bows and arrows of Virginia Indians. The Nansemond Fort is a per-fect case study. This large bastioned fort was built in an area where there was a major risk of attacks by the Nansemond Indians and little reason to be concerned about a Spanish incursion. In contrast, the primary objec-tive of Martiau's Hornwork was not to ward off Virginia Indians, who by the 1630s had been driven out of the eastern part of the Lower Peninsula, but to defend against an European artillery attack whose cannon balls would have made kindling out of the thin wooden walls of palisaded forts.

Virginia Company of London officials were quite aware of this vital distinction between these two different types of defenses, remarking at a meeting on March 2, 1620:

> "…signefyinge of two sortes of ffortefycacons, one for the induringe
> of assaults and Battery, which is not as hee Accompts there very
> needful butt rather the other of chusinge and takinge some place of
> Advantage, and there to make some Pallysadoes…" [35]

The word "Battery" in this passage meant the demolition of masonry fort walls by the battering of concentrated cannon fire. By the 17ᵗʰ cen-tury, the standard method to defend against "battery" included building geometrically designed forts with angled bastions and outworks, as ex-emplified by the Yorktown hornwork. The trapezoidal forts at Nansemond and Wolstenholme Towne, on the other hand, in many ways resemble the fortified compounds of English colonial settlements in Ireland. [37] The fact that most early Virginia forts bear little affinity to contemporary Euro-pean fortification practice suggests that they were an adaptation or ver-nacular development, perhaps based on Irish precedents, in military architecture primarily meant to deter Native American bowmen and not European artillery bombardments.

The hornwork found in Yorktown differs from all the other Virginia palisaded fortifications both in configuration and construction, and undoubtedly it was contrived by someone schooled in 17th-century military science, namely Nicolas Martiau. With this single exception, there isn't a hint that any of the other early Virginia forts or fortifications were designed by a professional military engineer. James Fort, however, was planned by professional soldiers who were veterans of the Low Country and, in some cases, the Irish wars. They assuredly drew on their experiences in deciding what type of fort to build in the Virginia frontier. James Fort, with its slot trench palisade walls and earthen bulwarks, seems to be a hybrid. Unlike the trapezoidal form of the Wolstenholme Towne and Nansemond forts, triangular forts were constructed in the late 16th and 17th centuries in Europe and Ireland.[36] Further, the presence of buttressing postholes along the inside of the riverside wall of James Fort—support posts not seen at any of the other palisaded fortifications—indicates that James Fort's walls were substantially taller than the breastworks at the Clifts or Nansemond Fort. Despite several setbacks, James Fort ultimately proved successful, validating George Percy's 1607 observation that the defenses created by the Jamestown leaders "…made our selves sufficiency strong for these savages."[37]

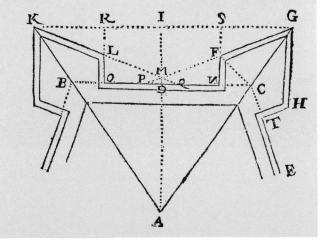

(18)

As in this figure let *B C* be the side of a Pentagon, whose angle at the Center is (by the 1. ch.　*B A C.*72. d.00.
the half whereof is　　　　　　　*C A D.*36.　00.
the complement thereof,　　　　*D C A.*54.　00.
now admit the angle of the bulwark,　*F G H.*69.　00.
the halfe thereof　　　　　　　*F G C.*34.　30.
subftraĉted from *S G c* being equall to　*D C A.*54.　00.
remaines the inward flanking angle　*S G F.*19.　30.
equall to *F P N* the compl. of either　*S F G.*70.　30.
subftraĉted from two right angles,　　　　180. 00.
leaves the angle of the fhoulder　*N F G.*109.　30.
Againe the fame angle *S F G* or　*I M G.*　70.　30.
doubled, gives the outward flan. ang.　*K M G.*141.　00.
Laftly from two right angles,　　　　180. 00.
subftr. half the angle of the poligon,　*B C A.*54.　00.
remaines the angle,　　　　　　*D C G.*126.　00.

Figure 42. Page from 1639 manual showing use of angles and proportions in fort design.

Figure 43. A 17th-century Dutch landscape depicting a Spanish olive jar in the lower right-hand corner. The jar still appears to be covered with the woven matting that protected it on the lengthy trip from southern Spain.

Chapter 4

by Beverly Straube

"Who is the Potter, pray, and who the Pot?"

Edward Fitzgerald
The Rubá'iyá't of Omar Khayyá'm

The large bulbous earthenware jar lies on its side next to the frozen Dutch river. Encrusted with the timeworn signs of neglect, it maintains frayed evidence of the woven straw covering which had protected it through its long voyage from the sunny lands to the south. Nearby, children strap on skates and a peasant climbs home with his load of wood, while men gather in front of the tavern on the hill. Perhaps, many months ago, these same men were the lucky imbibers of the contents of the jar— sweet wine from the Andalusian area of Spain. Now the jar, devoid of its contents and therefore uninteresting to the men, waits to be buried by the shifting soils of time.

If, centuries later, Dutch archaeologists should excavate the site of this mid-17th-century tavern scene, they may encounter sherds of the discarded jar by the river. Ceramic material, being of the earth, seems to form a symbiotic relationship with the soils that surround it. Unlike iron objects that rust away, glass materials that devitrify into splinters, and bone or wood artifacts that rot into mush, pottery will endure. The sherds may break apart and get smaller as nature or the effects of man move them around, the glazes may begin to separate from the fabrics, but the wares will still be identifiable.

Ceramics have been used throughout history to ship, store, prepare, and consume food and beverage. In addition, they have functioned to provide heat and light and, often, to reflect status. The role of pottery in the everyday social and economic systems of people subjects it to frequent breakage and disposal, but its relative durability ensures that it will survive in the ground. Ceramics become one of the most valuable classes of artifacts excavated by archaeologists, for they can reveal information about date, status, function, trading patterns, changes in eating or drinking habits, and migrations of populations.

This said, it must be mentioned that ceramics are all but invisible in the historical record. They are rarely listed on probate inventories and, if so, only in general terms. Shipping and customs records seem interested in ceramics only secondarily, as containers of goods. Indeed, there are no references in English importation records of pottery being the sole or most important cargo. "It always seems to have been one of the less important elements of mixed shipments."[38] It is up to archaeology to help fill in the gaps in our knowledge about ceramics.

The *Jamestown Rediscovery* excavations have uncovered over 20,000 fragments of pottery since 1994. Most of these sherds are from contexts dating to the first few years after settlement in 1607, and they represent wares from all over the world. The colonists did not attempt pottery production in Virginia until the 1630s, so before that time they had to rely on vessels produced elsewhere to meet their ceramic needs. Besides England, the countries of origin represented in the *Jamestown Rediscovery* ceramic assemblage are China, France, Germany, Italy, the Netherlands, Portugal, and Spain. What can these silent, sometimes colorful, objects tell us about the past? Why, for instance, are the English colonists using objects from Spain at the same time that they are building fortifications in anticipation of a Spanish attack? How does a small Chinese porcelain vessel link Jamestown with another Jamestown on an island off the coast of Africa, and thereby the Dutch trading monopoly with the East? What does a German count who was instrumental in the political play foreshadowing the Thirty Years War have to do with Jamestown?

These and other questions will be addressed in the following brief review of a few of the many interesting ceramics that have been excavated during *Jamestown Rediscovery's* excavations of James Fort.

Spanish OliveJars

The discarded jar lying in the corner of Isack van Ostade's painting, "A Winter Scene," is known by archaeologists and ceramic historians as a Spanish olive jar. This term, coined by American anthropologist William Henry Holmes in the beginning of this century,[39] is rather misleading because it is known that these cheap and durable containers were not reserved just for olives. Oil, wine, water, pitch, turpentine, vinegar, honey, rice, beans, capers, chick peas, almonds, and even lead bullets are documented as having been shipped in these earthen vessels. "In general it would be safe to say that the jars served to carry almost anything that would go through the narrow mouth."[40] Nevertheless, the term *olive jar* is maintained in common usage because of its widespread recognition among archaeologists and ceramic historians.

References to the same vessels in Spanish historical documents describe them as *botijas peruleras,* or " jars of the New World." The term reflects the large-scale production of these earthenware containers beginning in the late 16th century that coincided with Spain's thrust to settle and exploit the Americas. They have been found on "every area visited by the Spaniards during their global explorations, from the South Pacific, throughout the New World empire, to Atlantic islands."[41] Spain kept her colonies totally dependent for goods and thereby was able to supplement profits derived from the imported commodities, including precious metals and gems, with extensive exports of staples. The "jars of the New World" were produced to ship, store, and distribute the vast quantity of commodities needed by the emerging Spanish colonies in the Americas.

Figure 44. Diego Velázquez, The Waterseller, 1619-1620. Spanish olive jars were made of the same earthenware fabric as the water jar in the foreground. These unglazed vessels allowed for some condensation thereby serving to keep the contents cool.

Botijas largely replaced the more expensive wooden barrels and casks traditionally used to transport goods. Much of Spain's oak by this time had gone into Armada ship timbers and into the barrels provisioning the ships. This, plus the fact that cask wood required seasoning time to prevent fouling the provisions stored in them, resulted in much higher production costs for wooden containers.[42] The olive jar was a relatively cheap alternative that could be speedily produced and whose rounded form was well suited to shipboard transport. Not only did the egg-like structure of the jar result in a sturdy vessel able to survive extremely rough treatment, but the rounded sides saved precious space aboard ship by fitting closely against the curving hulls.[43]

There are three types of 17th-century olive jars, which vary from one another in shape and rim formation. Two of the types, A and B, have been found on Jamestown vicinity sites dating to the first half of the 17th century. Type A reflects a large oblong shape and is primarily a container for wine or water.[44] The capacity of a Type A jar is about 17.85 liters and is thereby capable of holding the Castilian wine *arroba*, the standard unit of measurement for wine of just over 16 liters.[45] There have been no Type A jars found among the Armada shipwrecks, which supports the documentary evidence that wine rations for the Armada were not accounted in *arrobas* and were probably stored in casks.

There is also a volume relationship with the smaller, globular Type B olive jar. It was most commonly used for oil, which corresponds with its capacity to contain half the Castilian oil *arroba* of 12.56 liters.[46] Type C, which has not been found at Jamestown, is elongated and carrot-shaped and corresponds most closely to the old Cuban *cuartilla* of 2.28 liters.[47] Honey was traditionally sold in these smaller sizes.[48]

All three types have constricted necks and thickened rims that are tapered internally to take a cork. Corks on jars that needed frequent opening and closing may have been secured to a string that tied around the jar's neck as shown in Velasquez's 1618 painting, *The Waterseller*. While the depicted vessel is flat-bottomed with a handle, the top reflects the olive jar shape and it appears to be the same fabric. There is archival evidence that after some jars were filled, the cork stopper was sealed with pitch (*pez de Avila*) or plaster (*enyesso*).[49] Both underwater archaeology and historical records indicate that the jars were covered with woven matting of esparto grass to the mouth or with a latticework of twisted string. The former would have provided protection during the stacking and shipping of the vessels and perhaps incorporated, like the twisted string, a carrying loop.

Most of the olive jars found on Virginia sites are believed to have been made in Triana, the famed potter's section of Seville, although no kiln sites have been identified there.[50] The vessels were wheel thrown but hastily made, as evidenced by the numerous air pockets visible in the fabric and the clay droppings often trapped on the interiors of the vessels. The fab-

Figure 45. Wad of fired clay from Pit 3, in the same fabric as the Spanish oli ve jars. It probably fell into the opening of a jar as excess clay while the potter was finishing the neck.

ric ranges in color from light brown to pinkish tan, and often exhibits a light gray inner core. Sometimes there is a thin white coating on the exterior of the Sevillian olive jars, which may be a result of salt in the clay or water used in the potting process. Upon firing, salts migrated to the surface of the pots as moisture evaporated, creating a patchy whitish surface.[51]

Only four nearly complete Spanish olive jars have emerged from over 300 sherds of the ware excavated from James Fort thus far. Three are from Pit 4, dating ca. 1610. They are the Type A jars, and two have doughnut-like, thickened rims reflecting a semi-triangular shape. The rim of one of the jars is impressed with a circular mark containing a single incised line. Marks, both stamped and incised, have been found on jar necks from shipwrecks dating from the late 16th century to the 1640s. The marks could be the insignias of the makers of the jars, but the evidence, such as religious symbols indicating supply to a Catholic church and marks which correlate between olive jars and silver bullion in the same wreck, indicates that the stamp conveys ownership. This would suggest that the jars were meant to be reused in the transatlantic trade to bring more commodities to the owner.[52]

Figure 46. Large Type A olive jar from Pit 4, ca. 1610.

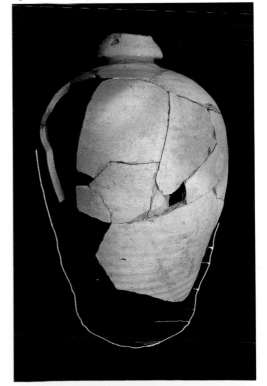

Some olive jars have been found with incised markings on their shoulders. These symbols are usually applied after the jar has been fired and are most likely potters' marks. They would be obscured by the grass matting fitted over the jars and would be of no use in signaling routing to intended recipients.

As mentioned earlier, this type of jar was the standard container for wine. Wine was a highly desired beverage in the colony, as was beer and aqua vitae. Water, which was

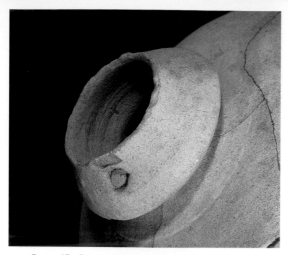

Figure 47. Stamped and incised owner's mark on the neck of a Type A olive jar from Pit 4.

often fouled, was consumed only as a necessity. If you could afford not to drink water, you wouldn't, as John Smith observed when he stated that "few of the Upper Planters drinke any water."[53] Beer quickly spoiled in the Virginia heat so wine was the drink of choice, and the estimated daily requirement for each colonist was at least one pottle [2 quarts] a day.[54] But wine was expensive, as it was an English import from Spain and France and therefore was not regularly supplied to the colony by the Virginia Company. According to John Smith "but one Hogshead [64 gallons] of Claret" was sent during the first three years.[55]

The fourth olive jar recovered from *Jamestown Rediscovery* was found within a ditch in the fort and is a Type B jar, traditionally used to ship oil. Oil was an important foodstuff for the colony, with each man to be allotted "1 gallon of oyle" per year.[56] Oil was used in cooking but also as a dressing with vinegar on green salads. An English cookbook dated 1596 instructs that "to make a Sallet of all kinde of hearbes" one should "mingle them with Cowcumbers or Lemmons payred and sliced, and scrape Suger, and put in vineger and Oyle."[57] Oil was obviously a very precious dietary substance to the colonists for Edward-Maria Wingfield, first president of the colony brought "2 glasses [bottles] wth sallet oyle" for his personal use from England and had them buried in the ground "so it wouldn't spoil."[58]

So where did the Jamestown colonists get their prized wine and oil represented by the discarded olive jars in James Fort? Before 1616 all the supplies to the colony had to come through the Virginia Company.[59] After this date private individuals could freely send supplies to their friends and relatives at Jamestown. In 1623, for instance, Robert Bennett received a shipment "out of Spain" from his brother, a London merchant. It included specialties from southern Spain, among them "19 Buttes of exclent good wynes, 750 jarse of oylle, 16 Barelles of Resones of the Sonne (raisins)" along with hogsheads of almonds and olives, all specialties from

Figure 48. Type B olive jar from Ditch 7, ca. 1630.

southern Spain.[60] However, in 1610, the contextual date of the Pit 4 jars, supplies were still strictly controlled by the Virginia Company. Even though trade between Spain and England had resumed 6 years earlier with the Treaty of London, it is very unlikely that the Company would supply such an expensive commodity to its colony. The most likely answer for colonists possessing Spanish olive jars is through trade, smuggling, or outright piracy in the Indies.

Stopovers for water and supplies in the West Indies were part of the route to Virginia for the English ships. The ships leaving London would sail south to the Canary Islands where they stopped to take on water before catching the northeasterly trade winds across the Atlantic to the Caribbean. This was the same route described by John Smith for the first settlers' voyage to Jamestown. They then spent three weeks in the "west-India Isles" refreshing themselves and trading "with the Salvages at Dominica." [61]

This was also the course used by the Spanish whereby, to reach their settlements, they entered the Caribbean Sea at the Windward Islands of Dominica and Guadeloupe. From almost the beginning of Spanish colonization of the New World there was the constant presence of English, French, and Dutch pirates and privateers preying on Spanish trading ships and settlements. Peace between England and Spain in 1604 put an end to

Figure 49. French marauders pillaging a Spanish colony in the Americas. At least two of the men are cradling olive jars in their arms as they hurry toward the waiting boat.

the officially commissioned piracy, at least by the English. But this did not stop the Dutch who continued their marauding, "sometimes with veteran English privateering veterans at the helm," until the mid 17th century.[62] There was persistent illegal trafficking of goods from Spanish settlements and ships resulting in a lot of Spanish wares floating around in places for which they were not intended.

One possible source of the Jamestown olive jars was recorded in 1608. At that time, Samuel Argall arrived at Jamestown on a fishing expedition for sturgeon "with a ship well furnished, with wine and much other good provision." The supplies had not been consigned to the colonists but were intended for private trade. Nevertheless, conditions were so bad at Jamestown that John Smith admitted, "though it was not sent us, our necessities was such as inforced us to take it."[63] Argall, following the traditional route to Jamestown, probably came by way of the Indies and quite possibly procured his cargo of wine through illicit commerce with Spanish settlements there, either directly or through Dutch privateers.

Martincamp

Whereas the Spanish olive jars were produced and shipped as containers for various substances, earthenware flasks from France were exported empty. Well over 400 neck and body pieces of these flasks, known as Martincamp, have been found in the *Jamestown Rediscovery* excavations, and they have been excavated from Virginia and Maryland sites dating to the first half of the 17th century. Martincamp flasks must have been produced solely for export, as they are rarely found in France but are very common on 16th and 17th-century sites in England where distribution clusters along the eastern coast and the eastern half of the southern coast. In London they are found most frequently in 17th-century contexts with the highest concentration ca.1650-1700. Surprisingly, no examples have been recognized in the Low Countries.

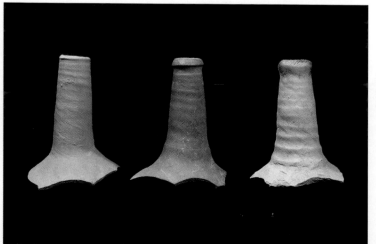

Figure 50. Martincamp flask necks from Pit 4, ca. 1610.

Martincamp is a village in northern France situated between Dieppe and Beauvais. The flasks were named Martincamp because it was believed that this was where the kilns were located. Now, ceramic historians believe that this attribution is too restrictive and that the ware may have been produced in a much wider area. Substantiating this belief is the fact that the Martincamp area has yielded neither large numbers of these flasks nor wasters.[64] Wasters are defective vessels that are unusable, generally through firing flaws, and are therefore discarded. They usually abound on kiln sites, providing the archaeologists with valuable information on the date and origin of wares.

Three distinct fabrics have been identified for Martincamp flasks.[65] Type I flasks are earthenware with a date range of 1475-1550. Type II flasks are stoneware and are commonly found in the 16th century. Type III, which is rounder in form than the previous two types, is the variety found at Jamestown. It has an earthenware fabric which usually is a low-fired orange color, but it can be fired to near stoneware and appear reddish orange.

Although other forms—rotund pots, chamber pots, and costrels—have been identified with the same fabrics in France, the only form found in Virginia is a thinly potted globular flask with a long tapering neck. The flask is wheel thrown into a sphere. Once the sphere is leather hard, the neck, which was thrown separately, is applied over a hole crudely punched in one end.

Martincamp flasks were seemingly exported empty to serve as canteens for field workers and soldiers. This has been deduced from studying 16th- and 17th-century English port books, which record values of cargo for tax purposes.[66] The flasks, described in the Port Books as "earthen bottles," are very inexpensive compared to the glass bottles that were exported from France with them. The low cost plus the lack of mention of any contents, which would have been subject to duty, suggest that the flasks were empty.

Figure 51. Complete Martincamp flask excavated from the site of Samuel Champlain's early 17th-century settlement in Quebec.

Figure 52. The wicker-covered bottle in this painting is probably made of glass but it reflects the same shape as wickered earthenware flasks from Martincamp.

The flasks would work quite well as water containers because they were fired to a near-stoneware consistency. They could hold liquid, but since they were unglazed there would be some seepage causing condensation that would serve to keep the contents of the vessel cooler. In addition, the rounded shape of the vessel, like the egg-shaped olive jar, provided a form that could withstand more abuse without breaking. The only apparent problem as a field flask is transport, since there are no handles. Customs documents provide an answer to this question as well. Martincamp flasks are identifiable as the "bottles of earth covered with wicker" imported from French ports.[67] Italian glass wine bottles reflecting the same rounded shape as the flasks are also encased in wicker at this time. The wicker covering on the glass bottles was to protect the wine from exposure to the ruinous effects of light. On the flasks, it would provide a way for attaching a means of suspension so the vessel could be easily slung across a shoulder. In addition, a standing ring of wicker woven at the rounded base of the flask furnishes the means for the flask to stand upright, thereby making it a costrel.

North Italian Marbled Slipware

Earthenware costrels from Italy are found occasionally on 17th-century Virginia sites. A costrel has a long narrow neck with either a rounded or baluster-shaped body on a turned foot. Unlike the Martincamp flasks, it has integral attachment lugs, often in the shape of stylized lion heads, on each side of the body through which cordage can be looped. A slip-decorated earthenware, the costrels are made of the red-firing alluvial clays of northern Italy, particularly the Pisa area. In the 16th and 17th centuries this area was the largest producer of exported Italian pottery, with its wares distributed through the Mediterranean, northwest Europe, and the Americas.[68]

Figure 53. The North Italian Marbled Slipware costrel to the right would be used, just as the nearby wickered glass bottle, for decanting wine to the Venetian-style wineglasses in the basket. A braided cord is looped through the lugs on the costrel's body to serve as a handle.

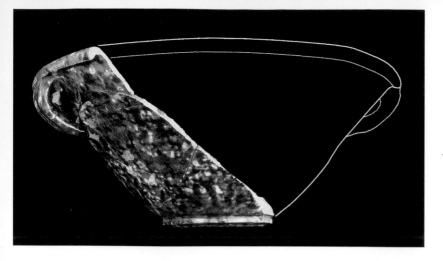

The ware is named North Italian Marbled Slipware, as two or more colors of slip-liquid clay are swirled together to present a marbled appearance on the surface of the vessel. The colors can be a mix of just white and red or include a polychrome palette of orange, brown, white, and green.

North Italian slipwares were also produced in the form of dishes and bowls, with the latter comprising the most common exports. A section of a very unusual bowl was recovered from the area within James Fort in a ca. 1625 context. It is very wide and is decorated on the interior and exterior with a dabbed, rather than swirled, white and red slip. Copper oxide in the glaze gives it an additional green mottled and streaked appearance.

Most interesting is the round-sectioned vertical handle applied to the body of the bowl, just under the rim. Presumably there was a second handle on the opposite side of the bowl, which is now missing. Adhering to the upper inside edge of the remaining handle is a fragment of what appears to be a second handle, which indicates that the bowl was a second, or imperfect vessel that was sold for use despite its defects. The handle fragment may represent what was meant to be a loose ornamental ring that adhered to the top of the handle while the vessel was fired upside down. If so, it is the first documented North Italian slipware use of this feature that is usually seen on 17th-century stoneware beakers from Dreihausen, Germany.[69]

While North Italian slipwares are widely distributed in Britain, they are not found in large quantities and are most heavily concentrated in London and coastal towns.[70] Examination of port records for these towns reveals a problem that can be encountered while attempting to define trading patterns based on the appearance of ceramics. The archival record shows little evidence of Italian shipping in English ports during the late 16th and early 17th centuries. Just because the wares are present does not mean that there is direct contact with their country of origin. Pottery is often sold and resold as it is imported and redistributed in foreign hands. Spain, for instance, is believed to be the intermediary between Italy and the Spanish colonial sites in the Americas, where North Italian Marbled Slipware has been found in contexts dating to the first half of the 17th century.[71] Spain is also thought to be responsible for the redistribution of the ware in the southern English port of Exeter during the late 16th and early 17th centuries.[72]

North Italian slipwares occur on Virginia sites dating to the second and third quarters of the 17th century, which is a context coinciding with intense Dutch trade with the English colonies. This commerce is believed responsible for the presence of these Italian wares on Virginia sites.

Chinese Porcelain

In 1613 the *Witte Leeuw (White Lion)*, a ship of the Dutch East India Company (V.O.C.), sank in Jamestown Bay during battle with two Portuguese merchant vessels. It was a Jamestown half a world away from the colony founded by Englishmen in the New World, but the two Jamestowns are inextricably linked by a diminutive porcelain cup made in China.

The site of the Dutch ship's sinking is in the waters of St. Helena, which is an island situated in the South Atlantic Ocean off the western coast of Africa. The *Witte Leeuw* had stopped at St. Helena to take on fresh supplies for the rest of her trip back to the Netherlands with a cargo of spices, diamonds, and porcelains from the East. This respite proved disastrous when two Portuguese carracks laden with goods from India chose the same protective anchorage. In the era's struggle for dominance in the eastern trade, the Portuguese and Dutch customarily sank or seized each other's ships, and this was no exception. An English eyewitness to the ensuing battle revealed that a cannon on the *Witte Leeuw* "broke over his Powder Roome…and the shippe blew up all to pieces."[73]

Figure 55. *Chinese porcelain wine cup from Pit 4 with flame frieze decoration.*

The shipwreck was excavated in 1976. Among the many artifacts recovered by archaeologists are over 300 complete or nearly complete Chinese porcelain vessels, plus an additional 300-400 kg of porcelain sherds. According to divers on the wreck, this probably represents only a quarter of the total porcelain cargo carried by the ship.[74] These findings are surprising for the ship's loading list made no mention of porcelain. Possibly, the vessels were the personal goods of the captain, officers, or passengers; but the sheer quantity of the material and the multiple copies of

form and decoration of the porcelain suggests that it was a cargo paid for and ordered by the Dutch V.O.C.

Comprising part of the porcelain assemblage are at least 40 small, thinly potted wine cups. Some are plain, but most are neatly painted in underglaze blue just above the footring with a band of scrolls under a flame pattern. "The shape is typical Chinese and resembles the well known wine cup or, in Japan, the sake-cup."[75] The wine cups are of the type known as fine porcelain and, until their recovery from the *Witte Leeuw*, it was not known that this quality of porcelain had been exported at such an early date. Fine porcelain in the early 17th century was customarily considered Imperial ware, reserved for use by the Chinese elite. Since the *Witte Leeuw* discoveries, however, these same wine cups have been recognized elsewhere—including another Dutch shipwreck, the *Banda*, which sank at Mauritius in 1615—thereby substantiating their use as export ware. The wine cups reached the Netherlands at least by 1617, as indicated by a Dutch still-life painting of that date depicting two of these vessels. The latest context in which these cups have been found is a 1640s shipwreck of a Chinese merchantman in the South China Sea, known as the Hatcher wreck.[76] Predating any of these examples is the nearly complete wine cup excavated from a ca.1610 context within James Fort.

More than a dozen more of these fine wine cups have been found on 17th-century archaeological sites along the James River near Jamestown. They do not appear to have been brought in one shipment, for there is a wide range of contexts (ca. 1610-1640) in which these vessels have been found. In addition, the cups from the latter part of the period have different characteristics indicating a typology. They are more heavily potted than the early examples, and the scroll and flame frieze appears slightly higher up on the body.

The wine cup at James Fort was most assuredly brought by, or sent to, one of the gentlemen in the colony. A gentleman's position in the colony was assured as much by the material goods he possessed and the way he dressed as by any inherited title. As a rare and expensive object, the Chinese porcelain wine cup would be quite fitting as a status indicator for an upper-class individual.

The wine cup may have been used to drink a strong alcoholic beverage, such as the aqua vitae that is listed as part of each colonist's provisions, or it may have just been for display. It was quite fashionable in the early 17th century among European nobility and upper classes to assemble cabinets of curiosities. These consisted of objects, collected around the world, which were scientifically interesting, exotic, or precious. "*Naturalia—objets trouvés* such as pearls and shells—were mixed quite happily with *arteficialia,* that is, precious man-made objects including coins, medals, paintings, sculptures, Nautilus goblets, astronomical gadgetry, etc."[77] Porcelains, often mounted in silver or gold, were often part of

Figure 56. A 1617 painting by Dutch artist Christoffel van den Berghe depicting Chinese porcelain wine cups with the flame-frieze motif (detail) like the wine cup from Pit 4.

these displays. In fact, a cabinet assembled between 1625 and 1631 for King Gustavus Adolphus II of Sweden contained three of the flame-frieze wine cups.[78]

The Jamestown wine cup was most likely part of a Dutch shipment of goods from the East that was traded in London. The English were doing very little trade with China, even after the foundation of the English East India Company in 1600. The Dutch wrested control of the East Indian trade from the Portuguese in the late 16th century and maintained it through the 17th century.

Raeren Stoneware

The fashionable woman in Floris van Schooten's 17th-century still life seems only mildly distracted by her son's appeal to play as she cleans fish in her well-stocked kitchen. It is obviously a well-endowed Dutch household, perhaps even modeled after the wealthy Haarlem artist's own.[79] Not only is there an abundance of food, but the metal cookware and the row of pewter plates behind three matching Chinese porcelain bowls all reflect an ability to invest in high-priced vessels for the preparation, storage, and consumption of food.

Hanging almost in shadow beneath the shelf of porcelain and plates are two blue and gray stoneware jugs mounted with pewter lids. These highly decorated baluster jugs were made in Raeren specifically for decanting into drinking vessels of glass or precious metal at the table. Primarily utilitarian, the jugs' intricate molded designs, derived from contemporary printed sources, propelled them into objects of conspicuous display. "Relief-decorated stoneware quickly became a medium of social competition among the emerging mercantile and artisanal classes of northern Europe."[80]

Raeren potters molded many different designs on the central panel of baluster jugs, including biblical and mythological scenes, details from popular contemporary prints, and armorial and political imagery. The important social role of these stonewares in European society contributed to their use, by potters and by the consumers who commissioned their wares, in conveying religious and political allegiances. "With the political and religious upheavals of the period, vessels decorated with the arms and portraits of contemporary rulers or historical figures were popular among gentry and mercantile class alike, both groups eager to display their fealty and political sympathies, even within the home environment."[81]

The two jugs in the van Schooten painting promote a political stance through a very popular motif known as the "Seven Electors." The seven Electors (*Kurfürsten*) comprised the Electoral College of the Holy Roman Empire. As such, they selected the emperor that ruled the Germanic dominion that encompassed most of central Europe and Italy. The pope was the spiritual head of the Empire that the German kings ruled from

*e 57. A Kitchen Scene by Dutch painter Floris van Schooten, showing Raeren
~ware jugs molded with the Seven Electors motif hanging in the background.
jugs are mounted with silver or pewter lids (inset), which increases their value
reveals their high status among the 17th-century tablewares.*

962 until 1806. While the position of emperor was
elective, by the 17th century it was solidly in the hands
of the Austrian Habsburgs, part of the Catholic dy-
nasty that commanded Spain, Portugal, a great deal
of Italy, and the southern Netherlands. The electors,
who were not all Catholic, were hereditary office
holders of the Empire and included the bishops of
Trier, Cologne, and Mainz, the King of Bohemia, the
Count Palatine of the Rhine, and the dukes of Saxony and Brandenburg.

Raeren potters produced "Seven Electors" jugs in the first 10 years of
the 17th century for export and domestic use. Judging by the examples that
have been excavated or that have survived in European museum collec-
tions, it was the most prevalently depicted theme on Raeren molded baluster jugs.[82] The design advertises political allegiance to the Habsburg-
ruled Holy Roman Empire at a time of abounding political-religious con-
flicts in Europe. Catholic-Protestant rivalries were rife even among the
German nation states of the Empire. Indeed, one of the electors, Count
Palatine of the Rhine, was a Calvinist who in 1609 encouraged the Prot-

Figure 58. Raeren stoneware "Seven Electors" jug from Ditch 1 within James Fort.

estant German states to form the Protestant Union. In response, the Catholic German states formed the Catholic League, supported by Spain, thus paving the way to the Thirty Years War.

The Netherlands comprised a particular area of turmoil as Spain attempted to prevail over the Dutch territories. Raeren's proximity to these military struggles explains many of the designs employed by the potters working there. Today, the village of Raeren lies in Belgium about 1 kilometer from the German border; but, during the peak of its stoneware potting industry 400-500 years ago, Raeren was a part of Germany located "on the edge of the territories known collectively as the Spanish Netherlands."[83] As the Raeren potters attempted to appeal to as large a market as possible, they produced equal numbers of wares bearing the coats-of-arms or symbols of Spain or the Habsburg family as those representing anti-Habsburg factions.

The base section of a Raeren "Seven Electors" jug was recovered from a ditch within James Fort. Only a tiny fragment remains of the mid-girth frieze which, if complete, would have consisted of the arcaded busts of the Seven Electors, each behind a shield bearing his hereditary coat of arms. The jug fragment has a rampant lion holding an orb, which is the coat of arms of the Count Palatine of the Rhine. The Palatine had its capital at Heidelberg and included strategically important land on both sides of the Rhine River between the Main and Neckar rivers. The Count Palatine from 1583 to 1610, when the stoneware jug would have been made, was Frederick IV, The Upright. Frederick IV practiced Calvinism, and it was he, who in 1609, instigated formation of the Protestant Union.

If the Electors jug was designed to advertise political loyalty with the Spanish-Habsburg dominion, what is it doing at Jamestown? The answer can perhaps be found in the policies of King James. A confirmed pacifist, one of James' first acts as king was negotiating the end of the Anglo-Spanish War with the controversial 1604 Treaty of London. Peace with Spain was driven by James' "desire for a dynastic union with Habsburg Spain as a mode of entry into the highest circle of European power and prestige."[84] His apparent Spanish sympathies emboldened Hispanophiles in the Ja-

Figure 59. If the coat of arms on the Raeren jug from Ditch 1 had been complete, it would have depicted the bust of the Count Palatine of the Rhine behind his coat of arms. In 1613 King James' daughter, Elizabeth Stuart, married Frederick V, the Elector Palatine and successor to Frederick IV, who is represented on the jug from James Fort.

cobean Court, such as the Earl of Northampton, to become more vocal in advancing Spanish and Catholic interests. Anti-Spanish groups, promoting an aggressive Protestant foreign policy, countered these actions. James had need for both and attempted to accommodate all factions in trying to forge alliances to strengthen his position. For instance, at the same time that his daughter married Protestant Elector Palatine, Frederick V, he was arranging for the union of his son with the Catholic Infanta of Spain.

In short, English foreign policy at the time of Jamestown's settlement was driven by the King's alignments with the royal houses of Europe amidst political and religious dissension. So, the English fortified themselves at Jamestown with a wary eye cast in Spain's direction while Spain kept track of every move of the Virginia venture through spies and counterintelligence. The Seven Electors jug would not be out of place in such an environment. It was probably owned by one of the gentlemen and was used or displayed to advertise his status in society. The jug was one of the symbols of a Jacobean gentleman who moved in courtly or upper class circles and affiliated himself with the strength and prestige of the Habsburgs, no matter what their religious leanings. One such gentleman was Edward-Maria Wingfield, first president of the council in Virginia. In his own words Wingfield sums up the contemporary conflicting views of the upper class in response to charges that he had colluded with Spain to the detriment of the colony:

> *"I confesse I haue alwayes admyred any noble vertue & prowesse, as well in the Spanniards (as in other nations); but naturally I haue alwayes distrusted and disliked their neighborhoode."*[85]

Frechen Stoneware

Another stoneware vessel recovered from within James Fort also contains iconography that is reflective of pro-Catholic sentiments. It is a brown salt-glazed jug from Frechen, a village to the west of Cologne, Germany. Frechen stonewares dominated the English market from the mid-16th century through to the late 17th century when the large-scale production of glass bottles and the development of English stoneware finally replaced them.

The jugs were primarily used for the storage and serving of beverages, a purpose for which they were ideally suited. The durable, non-porous stoneware body resulted in a vessel that could be easily cleansed of any odiferous substances and could contain liquids safely even under abusive circumstances. These stoneware jugs are often illustrated in Dutch tavern scenes sitting on the floor as a decanting vessel while the drinker consumes beer or wine from a glass.

The jug in Figure 61 is of the type known as *Bartmann* or "bearded man" for the bewhiskered face that adorns the neck. Bartmann jugs are also identified in the literature as "Bellarmines," a term popularly believed to be a satiric reference to the much despised Cardinal Robert Bellarmino (1542-1621). In 1606 Bellarmino, who was "a zealous opponent of Protestantism in the Low Countries and northern Germany," publicly rebuked King James I for his treatment of English Catholics.[86] While the association between the bulbous grimacing jug and the Catholic prelate may have

Figure 60. Bartmann jug standing by the feet of a soldier who is drinking beer from a glass. These durable stoneware containers quickly evolved in status to decanters that could be used at the table in conjunction with drinking vessels made of other materials.

Figure 61. Bartmann jug from Pit 1, ca. 1610.

been made by the English and Dutch during the tempestuous religious climate of the early 17th century, it is unlikely that the form originated as a caricature. The first *Bartmänner* were produced around 1550 when Bellarmino was only eight years old!

The Bartmann jug was excavated from Pit 1, a ca. 1610 context within the palisaded walls of James Fort. Besides its bearded mask with a curved ladder mouth, it exhibits parts of what would have been three ovoid medallions applied to its belly. Medallions on Bartmänner are often armorial reflecting the coats-of-arms of affluent patrons, European cities and royal houses, ecclesiastical offices, or even the potter's own *Hausmarke* or symbol.

The medallion on the Pit 1 jug consists of a crowned shield that has been divided into four quarters. In heraldic terms, the first and third quarters each exhibit a single lion *passant*, which means that he is walking with his right paw raised. The second and fourth quarters each have two lions passants. In the first quarter, which is the upper left-hand corner of the shield, there is a heraldic device known as a *fess with a label on chief.* This is the band across the upper third of the escutcheon that is carrying three stylized fleurs-de-lis. It is this label that identifies the medallion as Italian and, more specifically, as representing a member of the Tuscan Anjou party or Guelfs who from medieval times were staunch supporters of the Pope.[87]

The Guelfs' principal rivals in 13th-century Tuscany were the Ghibellines who backed the imperial power of the Holy Roman Emperor. These political factions had originated in Germany where they had comprised two feuding powerful families: the Wuelfs and the Hohenstaufen. The latter were the hereditary occupants of the imperial throne and once in Italy they, then known as the Ghibellines, had the support of the aristocracy. Artisans and lesser nobles characterized the Guelf party. It was a political struggle that was to divide Tuscany until 1282 when, with the support of the Pope who resented the threat of imperial authority in Italy, the Guelfs finally prevailed. They continued to be fiercely loyal to the papacy into the 17th century.

Guelf coats-of-arms have never before been recorded on German stoneware. Further, there is no documented trade of the ware in Italy so the Bartmann jug from Pit 1 is extremely rare. It must have been commissioned by an individual, perhaps an Italian merchant, who had trade or

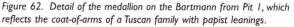

Figure 62. Detail of the medallion on the Bartmann from Pit 1, which reflects the coat-of-arms of a Tuscan family with papist leanings.

other contacts with northwest Europe. But what is the jug doing at Jamestown? While potters produced armorial stoneware with an eye to where it would be marketed, the places where heraldic medallions are found should not be strictly used to identify locations of individuals. Marketing practices of the international stoneware trade resulted in much random geographical distribution of armorial stoneware. Early 17th-century Frechen jugs found in England were, for the most part, purchased in bulk by Dutch merchants who then shipped them to London where they were redistributed to English markets.[88] The jugs changed hands many times as they were bought and resold thus resulting in widespread dispersal of motifs.

It may never be determined why this rare coat of arms with medieval connotations, showing Italian connections with the Rhineland and deference to papal authority, ended up at Jamestown. Was it the result of random distribution to a consumer oblivious to the jug's symbolism or was it a purposeful statement by one of the colonists with papist leanings?

This question, as well as many others posed by the ceramic assemblage from the *Jamestown Rediscovery* excavations, is opening up new areas of historical consideration that have not been posed by the written record. Every bit a primary source, as a letter or account written 400 years ago, each vessel has a story to tell if we only learn to decipher the codes.

Endnotes

[1] Map of Virginia, 1608, Archivo General de Simancas (Ministerio de Cultura de España), M. P. y D. IV-66.

[2] William Strachey, "A True Reportory of the Wreck and Redemption of Sir Thomas Gates, Knight," in A Voyage to Virginia in 1609, ed. Louis B. Wright (Charlottesville, VA: Univ. Press of Virginia, 1964), 79.

[3] Philip L. Barbour, ed., The Complete Works of Captain John Smith (1580-1631) (Chapel Hill, NC: The Univ. of North Carolina Press, 1986), II: 317-318.

[4] Strachey, 63-64.

[5] Alexander Brown, The Genesis of the United States (Cambridge: The Riverside Press, 1891), II:415.

[6] Strachey, 79.

[7] Barbour, II: 225; ibid., II: 189.

[8] Ibid., II: 187.

[9] Jamestown Land Patents, Book 2, 10-11, from the Virginia State Land Office, Richmond, VA.

[10] Algemeenrijksarchief's Gravenhage Colectie Leupe Supplement Velh, 619.89.

[11] Journals of the House of Burgesses, 1619-1659, Records of the Virginia General Assembly 1619-1978, 20.

[12] From the William Byrd Title Book, 1637-1743, Virginia Historical Society, Richmond, VA.

[13] British Public Records Office, High Court of Admiralty, Instance and Prize Courts, Examinations, May 25, 1650, High Court of Admiralty, Answers, 1656-58, Vol. I.

[14] Calvin Coolidge, address before the American Society of Newspaper Editors, January 17, 1925.

[15] Joel L. Shiner, Final Report, "Archaeological Explorations in the Confederate Fort Area in the APVA Grounds," Park Research Project No. 100 (Jamestown, VA: Colonial National Historic Park, 1955).

[16] For the history of Fort Raleigh, see David B. Quinn, Set Fair for Roanoke (Chapel Hill, NC: University of North Carolina Press, 1985). Ivor Noël Hume, The Virginia Adventure (New York: Alfred A. Knopf, 1994) contains an overview of all the archaeological excavations at Fort Raleigh.

[17] Nicholas M. Luccketti, "A Summary History and Report on the Archaeology at John Smith's New Forte," Discovery XV(1982): 2.

[18] J.C. Harrington, "Archaeological Exploration of the Area to be used for Sewerage Disposal Field in the Grounds of the Association for the Preservation of Virginia Antiquities, Jamestown Island," manuscript, United States Department of Interior, Colonial National Historical Park, Jamestown, VA, 1949.

[19] There are several other Virginia archaeological sites that may have some form of fortification that were not included in this discussion. The Hallowes Site almost certainly was a fortified house; see William T. Buchanan and Edward F. Heite, "A Seventeenth-Century Yeoman's Cottage in Virginia," Historical Archaeology (1971): 5:38-48 and Charles T. Hodges, "Private Fortifications in 17th-century Virginia," in Theodore R. Reinhart and Dennis J. Pogue, ed., The Archaeology of 17th-Century Virginia, Special Publication No. 30 (Richmond, VA: Archaeological Society of Virginia, 1993). Excavation of the ca.1619 Jordan's Journey settlement in Prince George County has produced evidence of a post-rail-and-plank enclosure around the main site, but whether this was simply a fence or some type of simple fortification is very problematical; see Douglas C. McLearen and L. Daniel Mouer, Jordan's Journey III, Virginia Commonwealth University Archaeological Research Center for the Virginia Department of Historic Resources, Richmond, VA, 1994.

[20] A discussion of punches and puncheon construction can be found in Cary Carson, Norman F. Barka, William M. Kelso, Garry Wheeler Stone, and Dell Upton, "Impermanent Architecture in the Southern American Colonies," Winterthur Portfolio, 16:2/3 (1981).

[21] The results of the archaeological excavations at Wolstenholme Towne are published by Ivor Noël Hume, Martin's Hundred (Charlottesville, VA: University Press of Virginia, 1991).

[22] The history and archaeology of Flowerdew Hundred can be found in James Deetz, Flowerdew Hundred, (Charlottesville, VA: University Press of Virginia, 1993).

[23] Hodges, 189.

[24] Deetz, 32-33.

[25] The salvage excavations were conducted under the auspices of the Yorktown Archaeological Trust and directed by Garrett Fesler and Nicholas Luccketti.

[26] A history of Nicolas Martiau can be found in John Baer Stoudt, *Nicolas Martiau, The Adventurous Huguenot* (Norristown Press: 1932). It unfortunately does not include citations.

[27] Susan M. Kingsbury, *Records of the Virginia Company* (Washington, D.C.: Government Printing Office, 1906), I: 317.

[28] Martha McCartney, "History of the Nansemond Fort Site," manuscript on file, APVA *Jamestown Rediscovery.*

[29] The Nansemond Fort site excavation was conducted by the Virginia Company Foundation, which is now a part of the APVA. The excavation was directed by Nicholas Luccketti and Garrett Fesler.

[30] The VRCA rescue excavations at Gloucester Point were carried out under the direction of David K. Hazzard.

[31] David K. Hazzard and Martha W. McCartney, "Rescue Efforts to Save the Vanishing Traces of Gloucester Town," *American Archaeology,* 6:1 (1987).

[32] Fraser Neiman was responsible for the fieldwork and analysis of the findings of the Clifts.

[33] Fraser D. Neiman, *The "Manner House" Before Stratford (Discovering the Clifts Plantation)* (Stratford Hall Plantation: Robert E. Lee Memorial Association, Inc., 1980); Fraser D. Neiman, *Field Archaeology of The Clifts Plantation Site, Westmoreland County, Virginia* (Stratford Hall Plantation: Robert E. Lee Memorial Association, Inc., 1980).

[34] Kingsbury, I:317.

[35] Ibid.

[36] For discussions of Irish precedents for Virginia fortifications, see John Reps, *Tidewater Towns* (Williamsburg, VA: The Colonial Williamsburg Foundation, 1972); Noel Hume, *Martin's Hundred*; and Hodges, "Private Fortifications."

[37] George Percy, *Observation Gathered out of "A Discourse of the Plantation of the Southern Colony in Virginia by the English, 1606,"* David B. Quinn ed. (Charlottesville, VA: The University Press of Virginia, 1967), 22.

[38] John Allan, "Some Post-Medieval Documentary Evidence for the Trade in Ceramics," *Ceramics and Trade*, Peter Davey and Richard Hodges, eds. (Sheffield:

University of Sheffield, 1983), 41.

[39] William Henry Holmes, *Aboriginal Pottery of the Eastern United States* (Washington, D.C.: 1903), 129.

[40] Mitchell W. Marken, *Pottery from Spanish Shipwrecks 1500-1800* (Gainesville, FL: University Press of Florida, 1994), 117.

[41] Florence C. and Robert H. Lister, *A Descriptive Dictionary for 500 Years of Spanish-Tradition Ceramics (13th through 18th Centuries),* The Society for Historical Archaeology, Special Publication Series, (1976), Number 1: 86.

[42] Laurence Flanagan, *Ireland's Armada Legacy* (Dublin: Gill and Macmillan, 1988), 106.

[43] Marken, 43.

[44] Ibid., 117.

[45] *Encyclopedia Universal Ilustrada,* (1910), 424 ; Colin J. M. Martin, "Spanish Armada Pottery," *International Journal of Nautical Archaeology and Underwater Exploration* 8.4 (1979): 284.

[46] Martin, 283-284.

[47] Marken, 125.

[48] Ibid., 137; George E. Avery, "Olive Jar Production, 16th-18th Century: A Multidisciplinary Approach," Paper presented at the Society for Historical Archaeology, Vancouver, Canada, (1994), 5.

[49] Ibid., 46-47.

[50] Martin, 281; Lister and Lister; Marken, 48.

[51] J. P. Benton et al, "Jericho tomb B47; a Palestinian Middle Bronze Age tomb in the Nicholson Museum," *Mediterranean Archaeology* (1993).

[52] Marken, 76.

[53] Barbour, III:216.

[54] Kingsbury, III:365-367.

[55] Barbour, III:271.

[56] Barbour, II:322.

[57] Thomas Dawson, *The Good Huswifes Jewell,* (London: 1596), Reprinted in *The English Experience* (Norwood, NJ: Walter J. Johnson, Inc., 1977), No. 865, D2-3.

[58] Jocelyn R. Wingfield, *Virginia's True Founder: Edward-Maria Wingfield and His Times 1550-ca.1614* (Athens, GA: The Wingfield Society, 1993), 338.

[59] Brown, 798.

[60] Kingsbury, IV:22.

[61] Barbour, II:137.

[62] Kris E. Lane, *Pillaging the Empire* (New York: Armonk, M. E. Sharpe, 1998), 57.

[63] Barbour, II:216-217.

[64] Pierre Ickowicz, "Martincamp Ware: A Problem of Attribution," *Medieval Ceramics*, (1993), 58.

[65] John G. Hurst, David S. Neal, and H. J. E. van Beuningen, *Pottery Produced and Traded in North-West Europe 1350-1650*, Rotterdam Papers VI (Rotterdam: Museum Boymans-van Beuningen, 1986), 103-104.

[66] Allan, 42.

[67] Ibid., 113; Denis Haselgrove, "Imported Pottery in the 'Book of Rates' English Customs Categories in the 16th and 17th Centuries" in *Everyday and Exotic Pottery from Europe, Studies in Honour of John G. Hurst,* David Gaimster and Mark Redknap, eds. (Exeter: Short Run Press, 1992), 327.

[68] Hurst et al, 30.

[69] David Gaimster, *German Stoneware 1200-1900* (London: British Museum Press, 1997), 299.

[70] David Crossley, *Post-Medieval Archaeology in Britain* (New York: Leicester University Press, 1990), 256.

[71] Kathleen Deagan, *Artifacts of the Spanish Colonies of Florida and the Caribbean 1500-1800,* Volume 1: Ceramics, Glassware, and Beads (Washington, D.C.: Smithsonian Institution Press, 1987), 47.

[72] Allan, 44.

[73] *Hakluytus Posthumus or Purchas his Pilgrims* (London: 1925), Vol. 1, as cited in C. L. Van der Pijl-Ketel, ed., *The Ceramic Load of the Witte Leeuw* (Amsterdam: Rijksmuseum, 1982), 19.

[74] Ibid., 25.

[75] Ibid., 143.

[76] Julia B. Curtis, "Chinese Ceramics and the Dutch Connection in Early Seventeenth Century Virginia," *Vereninging van Vrienden der Aziatische Kunst Amsterdam*, 1:6.

[77] Norbert Schneider, *Still Life*, (Cologne: Benedict Taschen, 1994), 158.

[78] Van der Pijl-Ketel, 28-29.

[79] Ingvar Bergstrom, *Still Lifes of the Golden Age* (Washington D.C.: National Gallery of Art, 1989), 123.

[80] Gaimster, 143.

[81] Ibid., 153.

[82] Gisela Reineking von Bock, *Steinzeug* (Cologne: 1986), 273.

[83] Gaimster, 224.

[84] John Reeve, "Britain and the World Under the Stuarts," *The Oxford Illustrated History of Tudor & Stuart Britain,* John Morrill ed. (New York: Oxford University Press, 1996), 416.

[85] Wingfield, 337.

[86] Gaimster, 209.

[87] John Hurst, personal communication, 1997.

[88] Gaimster, 82.